The Complete Guide To
Glues & Adhesives

Nancy Ward & Tammy Young

Published by

krause publications

700 East State Street • Iola, WI 54990-0001
715/445-2214 • FAX: 715/445-4087   www.krause.com

Please call or write for our free catalog of publications. Our toll-free number to place an order or obtain a free catalog is 800-258-0929 or please use our regular business telephone 715-445-2214 for editorial comment and further information.

Library of Congress Catalog Number 99-69489
ISBN 0-87341-820-4

The authors and publisher have made every effort to ensure that all information and instructions given in this book are accurate and safe, but they accept no responsibility or liability for any injury, damage, or loss resulting from misuse or abuse of any product. The user is responsible for reading and following manufacturer's directions on all products, especially those which are flammable or contain dangerous solvents.

Registered trademarks are used only in an editorial fashion and to the benefit of the trademark owner; there is no intent to infringe upon a trademark. Product names are in italics; ™ and/or ® markings are not noted with company, brand, or product names.

Dedication, from Nancy

*This book is dedicated with love to my sons,
Jack, Dave, Tim, Joe, and Andy Gillen*

Preface

Since *The Crafter's Guide to Glues* was written in 1995, crafting activities have grown in scope and interest. Glue and adhesive manufacturers have done an outstanding job in keeping pace with these activities. Without exception, crafters now have an adhesive product suited for every type of project they might consider.

Originally, this book was intended as a revision, but it quickly became apparent that a completely new book would be needed in order to adequately provide the necessary information.

This change in the original plan presented problems for Tammy. Prior commitments did not allow her the time necessary for research, testing, and writing the new book. She asked me to step in and pick up where she left off. At the time, neither of us realized just how much new information would have to be included.

As in the first edition, this book is intended to lead you through the decision-making process when selecting an adhesive for your projects. The choices include the standard favorites, specialty adhesives, and many new products.

Every attempt was made to provide you with current information. Technology is mushrooming, creating exciting new frontiers for crafting, as well as other areas in our lives. To keep abreast of those new products, read magazine ads, check craft store displays, and visit adhesive company websites on the Internet.

Happy crafting!

Nancy Ward

Acknowledgments

Every book requires the efforts of several people. Three who contributed greatly to this book are Amy Tincher-Durik, Sue Bell, and Joyce Whipple.

Sincere thanks are due to the following companies. Without their cooperation and support, this book would not have been possible.

Products mentioned in the book are in italics and preceded by either the brand or company name; refer to that name in this listing. There are a few products that precede the company name; product names are in italics in those cases also.

3L Corp. (www.3l.dk)
3M 800-364-3577
Aabbitt Adhesives, Inc. (www.aabbitt.com);
    773-227-2700 or 800-AABBITT
Accent Export-Import, Inc.
    (www.fimozone.com); 800-989-2889
Accu-Cut Systems (www.accucut.com);
    402-721-4134
Activa Products, Inc.
    (www.activa-products.com); 800-255-1910
Adhesive Technologies, Inc.
    (www.adhesivetech.com/craft.htm);
    800-544-1021, ext. 123
Aleene's (www.duncancrafts.com/crafts);
    559-291-4444 or 800-237-2642
Amaco: See American Art Clay Co., Inc.
American Art Clay Co., Inc. (www.amaco.com);
    317-244-6871 or 800-374-1600
American Traditional Stencils
    (www.amtrad-stencil.com); 603-942-9957 or
    800-278-3642
Anita's (www.backstreetcrafts.com);
    678-206-7373
Art Accents (http://www.artaccents.net);
    877-733-8989 (orders only)
Artistic Woodworking (www.artwood.com);
    308-882-4873 or 800-621-3992
Artifacts. Inc. 903-729-4178
Avant'CARD (www.magicmesh.com)
Art Institute Glitter, Inc.
    (www.artglitter.com/index.html);
    520-639-0805 or 877-909-0805

B & B Etching Products, Inc.
    (www.etchall.com); 888-382-4255
Back Street, Inc. (www.backstreetcrafts.com);
    678-206-7373
Beacon/Signature
    (www.beacon1.com/craft.htm);
    973-427-3700 or 800-865-7238
THE BEADERY Craft Products/Green Plastics
    Corporation (www.thebeadery.com);
    401-539-2432
Bellarosa Paper Arts
    (www.bellarosapaperarts.com);
    218-879-1134
Bemiss-Jason Corp. (www.bemiss-jason.com)
Bond Adhesives Co. (www.coolbonder.ch);
    800-879-0529
Books by Hand 505-255-3534
Bostik
    (www.bostik.com/distribution/dist-index.html)
Cache Junction/Seitec 800-999-1989
Clearsnap, Inc. (www.clearsnap.com);
    800-448-4862
Clotilde (www.clotilde.com/store/);
    800-545-4002
Clover Needlecraft, Inc.
    (www.clover.co.jp/pw&q/01home.html);
    800-233-1703
Collins/Prym-Dritz (www.dritz.com)
Colozzle (www.coluzzle.com); 801-373-6838 or
    800-563-8679 (orders only)
ColArt Americas, Inc.
    (www.winsornewton.com)
Come Quilt With Me, Inc. 718-377-3652
CPE, Inc. (www.cpe-felt.com); 864-429-7900 or
    800-327-0059
Crafter's Pick/API (www.crafterspick.com);
    510-526-7616
Craf-T Products, Inc. (www.craf-tproducts.com)
Createx Colors (www.createxcolors.com);
    860-653-5505 or 800-243-2712
Daige Rollataq
    (www.daige.com/permhand.htm);
    516-621-2100 or 800-645-3323
Darice (www.darice.com)
DecoArt
    (www.decoart.com/0000/INDEX.HTM);
    606-365-3193

Delta/Delta Technical Coatings, Inc.
(www.deltacrafts.com); 800-423-4135
Design Innovations, Inc.
(www.claystamp.com); 415-922-6366
Dr. Ph. Martin's (www.docmartins.com);
954-921-6971
Dritz/Prym-Dritz (www.dritz.com)
Duncan/Duncan Enterprises
(www.duncancrafts.com); 559-291-4444 or
800-237-2647
Eclectic Products. Inc.
Elmer's Products, Inc. (www.elmers.com)
EK Success LTD (www.eksuccess.com)
etchall (www.etchall.com); 888-382-4255
FPC/Surebonder
(www.thomasregister.com/olc/fpccorp/);
847-487-4583
Fiskars, Inc.
(www.crafts.fiskars.com/crafts/index.html)
Frametek (www.frametek.com); 541-431-4365
or 800-229-9934
Frances Meyer, Inc. (www.francesmeyer.com)
Franklin International (www.titebond.com);
614-445-1493 or 800-877-4583 (technical
support)
Gane Brothers and Lane
(www.ganebrothers.com/Default.htm);
800-323-0596
General Pencil Company
(www.generalpencil.com/home.html);
650-369-4889
Genesis Artist Colors
(www.genesisartistcolors.com);
317-244-6871 or 800-374-1600
Germanow-Simon Corporation
(www.g-scorp.com/cement.html);
716-232-1440 or 800-252-5335
Green Sneakers (www.greensneakers.com)
Grafix (www.grafixarts.com)
Great Planes
(www2.towerhobbies.com/cgi-bin/WTI0095P);
217-398-3636 or 800-637-6050
HTC Inc. (www.htc-inc.net); 973-618-9380 or
888-618-2555
H. B. Fuller
Houston Art & Frame, Inc.
(www.houstonart.com)
J T Trading Corporation 203-339-4904
Jacquard Products
(www.jacquardproducts.com);
707-433-9577
Jim Stephan (jimstamper@mail.com);
760-382-8474
Jones Tones, Inc. (www.jonestones.com);
719-948-0048
Judi-Kins (www.judi-kins.com/index.htm);
310-515-1115
June Tailor (www.junetailor.com);
262-644-5288
K & S Engineering
(www.ksmetals.com/index.html)

Kiss-Off, Inc. (www.kissoff.com/main.html)
Krause Publications (www.krause.com);
715-445-2214
Krylon (www.krylon.com)
Lakeshore Plastics, Inc.
Lineco, Inc. (www.lineco.com)
Leech Products, Inc. (www.tapnglue.com);
800-992-9018
Lemon Tree (www.powderedpearls.com);
877-631-8028
Loctite Products (www.loctiteproducts.com);
800-321-0253
Lucky Squirrel (www.luckysquirrel.com);
505-861-5605
Magicalfaerieland
(www.magicalfaerieland.safeshopper.com);
206-367-2371
Magnaproducts 800-338-0527
Making Memories
(www.makingmemories.com);
800-929-7324
Manco, Inc. (www.manco.com); 800-321-0253
Mary's Productions (www.marymulari.com)
218-229-2804
McGill, Inc. (www.mcgillinc.com)
Moore Push Pin Co. (www.push-pin.com);
215-233-5700
Mostly Animals Corp.
(www.mostlyanimals.com); 209-848-2542
or 800-832-8886
MSI/Magnetic Specialty, Inc.
(www.magspec.com)
National Artcraft Co.
(www.nationalartcraft.com/index.html);
888-937-2723
Non Sequitor
(www.nonsequiturstamps.com/index.html)
NuCentury, Inc. (www.nucentury.net)
Off The Beaten Path (www.cookiecutter.com);
816-415-8827
Olfa (www.olfa.com); 800-962-OLFA
Paper Adventures (www.paperadventures.com);
800-727-0699
The Paperlady
(http://members.aol.com/sueperstuff/)
Paper Shops
(www.papershops.com/papershops/index1.html);
805-965-5574
Pamela Shoy Papers
(www.pamelashoypapers.com);
916-789-1025
Pioneer Photo Albums, Inc.
(www.pioneerphotoalbums.com)
Plaid/Plaid Enterprises, Inc.
(www.plaidonline.com); 800-842-4197
Polyform Products, Co. (www.sculpey.com)
Prairie Stamper
(www.prairiestamper.homestead.com);
701-743-4500
Provo Crafts (www.provocraft.com/index.php);
801-377-4311

Prym-Dritz Corporation
(www.dritz.com/index.html)
Purrfection Artistic Wearables
(www.purrfection.com/index.htm);
800-691-4293 or 360-653-0901 (outside U.S.)
Quick Grab, Inc.
(www.quickgrab.com/index.html);
978-374-0094
Ranger Industries, Inc. (www.rangerink.com)
Roo Products, Inc.
(www.rooglue.com/roowood.htm);
503-981-5640
Ross 800-387-5275
Royal & Langnickle (www.royalbrush.com)
Royal Brush MFG Co. (www.royalbrush.com)
Rupert, Gibbon & Spider, Inc.
(www.jacquardproducts.com);
707-433-9577 or 800-442-0455
Sailor Corp. Of America
Saunders/UHU U.S. distributor
(www.saunders-usa.com); 207-685-3385 or
800-341-4674
Satellite City 805-522-0062
Scotch 800-363-3577
Scratch-Art Company, Inc.
(www.scratchart.com); 508-583-8085
Scribbles
(www.duncancrafts.com/crafts/
scribbles/scribbles_home.htm);
559-291-4444 or 800-237-2642
Signature Crafts
(www.beacon1.com/index.htm);
941-699-3400
Specialty Tapes, Inc./TSI
(www.specialtytapes.net); 262-835-0748
Sueperstuff
(http://members.aol.com/sueperstuff/index.html)
St. Louis Trimming - Division of Trimtex Co., Inc.
Stewart Superior Corp.
(www.stewartsuperior.com)
STYROFOAM (www.styrofoam-crafts.com)
SureHold (www.surehold.com/welcome.html);
800-881-4495
Sue Gidduck
(http://members.aol.com/sueperstuff/)
Sulky Of America (www.sulky.com/index.htm);
941-629-3199
Sullivans USA, Inc,
(www.sullivans.net/usa/default.htm)
Sunday International
(www.sundayint.com/index.html);
800-401-8644
Suze Weinberg Design Studio
(www.schmoozewithsuze.com);
732-761-2400
Tecnocraft/Uniplast, Inc.
(www.uniplastic.com/consumer.htm);
817-640-3204

Therm-O-Boss
(www.thermoboss.com/index.html)
Therm O Web, Inc.
(www.thermoweb.com/consumer.html)
Think Ink (www.thinkink.net); 800-778-1935
Tombow (www.tombowusa.com/frame.html);
678-442-9224 or 800-835-3232
Tower Hobbies (www.towerhobbies.com);
217-398-3636 or 800-637-6050
TSI/Tape Systems, Inc.
(www.tapesys.com/rubberstamp.html)
Twinrocker Papermaking Supplies
(www.dcwi.com/~twinrock/Welcome.html);
765-563-3119 or 800-757-8946
Tulip
(www.duncancrafts.com/crafts/tulip/
tulip_products_home.htm); 559-291-4444
or 800-237-2642
UHU (www.saunders-usa.com); 207-685-3368
or 800-341-4674
UnDu Products, Inc. (www.un-du.com)
Uniplast, Inc.
(www.uniplastinc.com/consumer.htm);
817-640-3204 or 800-444-9051
University Products
(www.universityproducts.com);
800-336-4847
USArt Quest, Inc. (www.usartquest.com);
517-522-6225
Wallies, a division of McCall Pattern Company
(www.wallies.com); 800-255-2762, ext. 351
The Warm Company
(www.warmcompany.com/index.html)
What's New Ltd.
(www.whatsnewltd.com/index.htm);
480-830-4581
Winsor & Newton
(www.winsornewton.com/index.html)
Xyron. Inc. (www.xyron.com); 480-443-9419 or
800-793-3523
Yasutomo & Company (www.yasutomo.com);
650-737-8888
ZimInk (http://www.zimprints.com);
865-584-9430

Consult the websites of companies to keep informed of new products introduced following the publication of this book. In addition to product information, most sites provide projects with instructions, Material Safety Data Sheets (MSDS), and purchase sources for their products. Several also offer on-line purchasing.

If you do not have a home computer with Internet access, your local library probably has one for public use. If this is not practical, refer to the Resources; with very few exceptions, the products mentioned in the book are included in at least one of those mail-order or on-site catalogs.

Table of Contents

Chapter 1

The Basics

How a project will be used and the surfaces involved determine the adhesive best suited for it. Further, the category of adhesive you prefer, the amount of time required to apply it, and the time required for it to dry and cure have a great deal of impact on the type of adhesive to use for a certain application. Consider each of these factors, as well as others covered below, when selecting an adhesive.

End Use

We usually select a project by the way we intend to use it. Read the product's label or packaging to see if the type of project you are doing is included in the list of suggested uses and look for key words or terms that relate to your project. For instance, clothing requires a different type of adhesive than a scrapbook page, while decoupage doesn't need an adhesive that would be necessary for an outdoor decoration.

Surfaces

Surfaces, or substrates, are either porous, semi-porous, or non-porous. Very often, a product's container or packaging includes a list of recommended surfaces suitable for use with it. If you are using a product on surfaces not recommended by the manufacturer, test it before beginning your project to ensure satisfactory results.

Porous Surfaces

Porous surfaces are those that absorb liquids quickly and evenly. Examples include unfinished soft woods, uncoated paper, fabric, unfinished plaster, air-dry clay, and dried plant matter.

Semi-porous Surfaces

Semi-porous surfaces absorb liquids slowly and unevenly. They include sealed soft wood, hard wood, coated paper, treated fabric, craft foam, and sealed plaster.

Non-porous Surfaces

Non-porous surfaces are often slick and shiny and do not absorb liquids. Types of non-porous surfaces include painted or varnished wood, glossy paper, painted or varnished plaster, hard plastic foam, polymer clay, acetate, acrylic, glass, and metal.

Adhesive Categories

Adhesives are either water-based or solvent-based. Not all water-based adhesives include the words "water-based" on the label, yet federal law requires that solvent-based adhesives be clearly labeled with that information. Instructions for the proper use of those products also must be included on the label.

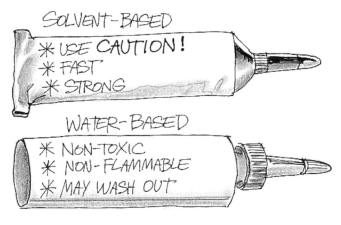

SOLVENT-BASED
* USE CAUTION!
* FAST
* STRONG

WATER-BASED
* NON-TOXIC
* NON-FLAMMABLE
* MAY WASH OUT

When Using Solvent-based Adhesives, Remember...

• These products require that you follow certain procedures during use; many are flammable. Read and follow all instructions on the label. After use, replace caps and tops tightly and store out of the reach of children. To ensure that warnings and instructions remain with these products, do not remove them from their original containers and place them in another.

• Under no circumstances should children use solvent-based products; they should use only those products labeled either "safe" or "suitable" for use by children.

• Pregnant women should avoid the use of solvent-based products, while nursing mothers and anyone with severe allergies should use extreme care when selecting products.

• The federal government requires that companies manufacturing glues and adhesives provide a Material Safety Data Sheet (MSDS) upon request. If you have any questions concerning the correct use of a product, or to determine if it may present a health problem for you, contact the company to obtain the product's MSDS.

Time

One or more of the following terms are often included on a label to inform you of the drying and curing times a product requires.

• **Open:** The time prior to set; repositioning of items is usually possible during this time.

• **Set or Setting:** The time required for an adhesive to become solid and stable.

• **Dry:** The time it takes for an adhesive to feel and look dry. Some glues dry clear, while a repositionable glue is dry when it feels tacky

and the surface is set. Humidity greatly affects drying time; what may take three hours to dry in Arizona could take as long as twelve hours in Mississippi. When possible, dry projects on some type of rack so air can circulate around all surfaces. A fan will hasten drying, and a hair dryer or heat gun can be used with some adhesives; use caution, though, because several adhesives soften when heated. Test to ensure satisfactory results.

• **Cure:** The amount of time required for complete bonding or adhesion. An adhesive that appears dry may not be completely cured. Prior to full cure, projects should remain in a stable position. It may be necessary to either clamp or secure adjoining pieces to hold them in position.

Plan Ahead Before Beginning

• **Finger and hand protectors:** Disposal plastic gloves are great for protecting your hands while using glues and adhesives. If you're a non-glove wearer, clean your hands as you go using pre-moistened wipes, a damp washcloth, or alcohol swaps. Alcohol swabs (available by the box in drugstores) are lint-free and also are handy to use for cleaning non-porous surfaces prior to applying an adhesive.

• **Work surface protectors:** Select protectors with care when using cements, super glues, and epoxies—these adhesives stick to many surfaces. Avoid the use of printed papers with ink that will bleed when wet because the ink will stain your project. A pad of newsprint is a good work surface; just remove the top sheet when it becomes messy. (Don't limit newsprint to this use; it's an excellent supply for many projects.) Non-stick surfaces include:
• Used plastic tablecloths and shower curtains cut to size.
• Cardboard wrapped with aluminum cooking foil.
• Cut pieces of either freezer wrap (plastic side up) or cooking parchment paper.
• Other non-stick surfaces described on page 11.

• **Drying and curing:** Determine before you begin where the project will be placed during the drying and curing period. If clamping is necessary, select the supplies needed. Some suggested items to use for drying and curing are:

• Plastic berry boxes (use these individually as a platform for small pieces, or connect several with twist ties when a larger area is needed).
• Cake cooling racks.
• Gizmo from a take-out pizza (looks like a tiny table).
• Metal "splatter" screen (used over frying pans) or plastic "splatter" screen (used in a microwave oven) placed over an empty cardboard box.
• Polyester batt "pillow" covered with plastic food wrap for cylindrical items.
• Long and regular-sized bobby pins for holding thin layers together.
• Clothespins.
• Large rubber bands.
• Clamps (like chip bag type or Bull Dog).
• Wooden skewers stuck upright in a *STYRO-FOAM* bar or sheet.

• **Read the project instructions.**

• **Gather supplies and tools** and read the labels on all supplies. Test if necessary.

• **Prepare the surfaces involved:** Wood may require sanding and/or sealing, while non-porous surfaces should be wiped with Isoprophyl (rubbing) alcohol, vinegar diluted with water, or a supply recommended on the adhesive's label. Regardless of the adhesive you have selected, all surfaces being bonded must be clean, dry, and free of oil and grease.

Although it seems that applying a large amount of an adhesive would result in a stronger bond, the opposite is usually true. In almost every case, **LESS IS BEST** is the key to successful bonding.

When burnishing is recommended, cover the surface being burnished with vellum or some other smooth, durable paper to avoid marking or damaging the surface.

To burnish, hold the edge of the burnishing tool firmly on the covered surface and pull the tool over all areas to which an adhesive has been applied. Depending upon the thickness of the surface being burnished, it may be necessary to make two or three passes over the surface. Items suitable for use as a burnishing tool include the edge of a charge card, the edge of a wooden ruler, a Clover Needlecraft, Inc. *Finger Presser*, a B & B Etching Products, Inc. etchall *squeegee*, and a Scratch-Art *Rubbing Stick*.

In some cases, weight also must be placed over surfaces until the adhesive has dried. Heavier items that cannot be burnished may require being clamped or tied in place.

When Finished

• **Clean-up:** Soap and water or a household cleaner will handle most spills and will clean most tools. Rinse foam brushes and sponges in water; a brush cleaner can be used on bristle brushes. After cleaning bristle brushes, reshape them and lay them flat until the bristles are completely dry. Store with the bristles up. Both rubbing alcohol and non-oily acetone polish remover do a good job of cleaning up most solvent-based adhesives. Use with caution—they also remove paint and varnish. Use either a damp kitchen sponge or damp paper towels to pick up spilled pigment powders, glitters, and embossing powders. Masking tape also picks up these spills, in addition to small beads, sequins, and spangles. *KissOff Stain Remover* removes most glue and paint from clothing; it also can be used to remove dried glue from brushes.

• **Storage:** Store adhesives out of direct sunlight, away from heat and cold. Replace lids and caps tightly. Place glues in applicator bottles with the tip down in a rack normally used in kitchen cupboards. Racks of this type also can be used as drying racks and are handy to use for storing tools, especially scissors.

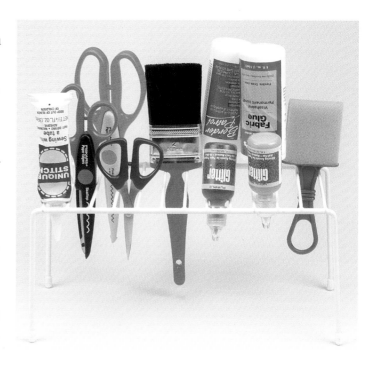

Timesaving Tools

The following photos are groupings of time-saving tools referred to throughout the book. Refer to these photos when the items are mentioned. You can, of course, substitute these with items of your choice.

Mixing Tools and Storage Containers
1. Small jar with lid
2. Plaid *Cubby Ware Container*
3. Craft sticks
4. Plastic dinnerware

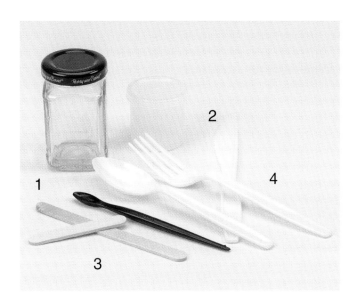

Palettes
Dried water-based adhesives lift easily from all plastic surfaces, including *Teflon* and *Mylar*; non-oily acetone polish remover, rubbing alcohol, or special removers may be required to remove some hot glues, solvent-based glues, and pressure sensitive adhesives from plastic surfaces.

1. What's New Ltd. *Magic Craft Sheet*
2. *Heavy-weight* and *Regular-weight Teflon Pressing Sheet* from Clotilde
3. *Heat Resistant Mylar Sheet* from Clotilde
4. Plastic lids from coffee cans and yogurt containers

5. Tecnocraft *Hot Glue Work Sheet*
6. Surebonder/FPC *Craft Work Surfaces*

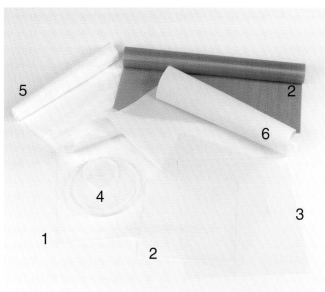

Applicator Tips, Bottles, and Syringes
These items are useful when applying an adhesive to a small area or in a bead. Remove the adhesive from the container after use and rinse out thoroughly.

1. Yorker-top bottle (purchase in crafts store)
2. etchall *applicator tips* and *bottles*
3. *Bottles and Tips Assortment* from Clotilde
4. Plaid *Tip Pen Set*
5. Aleene's *Glue Syringe*
6. Germanow-Simon Corp *G-S Cement Applicator*

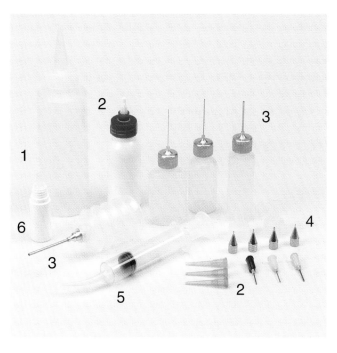

Burnishing Tools

1. B & B Etching Products, Inc. etchall *squeegee*: This multi-use tool can be used to smooth stencils to a surface, apply adhesives, remove excess adhesive, and for burnishing.

2. Scratch Art *Rubbing Stick*: When using this tool, position the bottom plate on the surface being burnished. A *Rubbing Stick* provides a faster method when larger areas are being burnished or when burnishing sheets of pressure sensitive adhesive or laminating film.

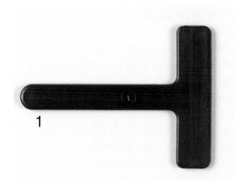

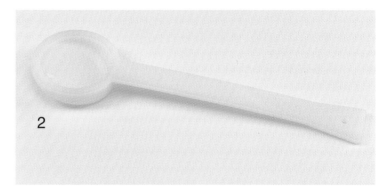

Brushes

1. Ross *Sponge Brush*
2. Royal Brush MFG Co. *Disposable Foam Brushes*
3. Plaid *Stippler Brush*: Use when making paste paper
4. Inexpensive bristle paintbrushes: Use when making paste paper
5. Royal Brush MFG Co. *Kid's Brush* in two sizes
6. Microbrush *Microbrushes* in two sizes

7. Royal Brush MFG Co. *Squeeze and Flo*: Diluted paste and glues (plain or colored) can be applied with this brush-top container when making paste papers
8. Royal Brush MFG Co. *Stippler Brush*
9. Flux brush (purchase at hardware store): Use for applying solvent-based adhesives
10. Royal Brush MFG Co. *Craft Inspirations Brush Assortment*: The end of the brush handles can be used to score paper for folding, as a stylus, and for burnishing small areas

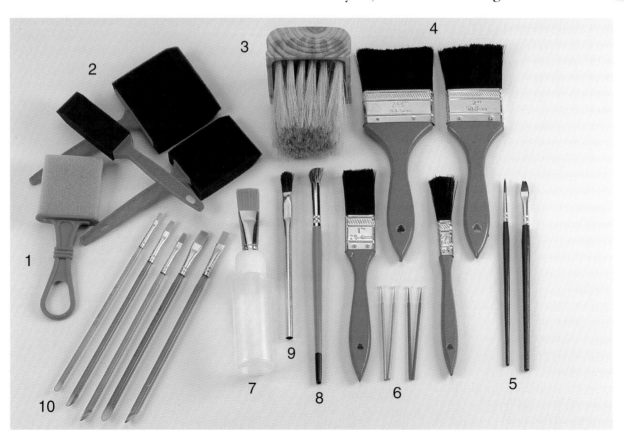

Rubber Brayers

A rubber brayer is used to apply a thin, even layer of adhesive or paint over a flat surface and also can be used for burnishing.

1 and 2. Scratch Art *Hard Rubber Brayer* and *Soft Rubber Brayer*

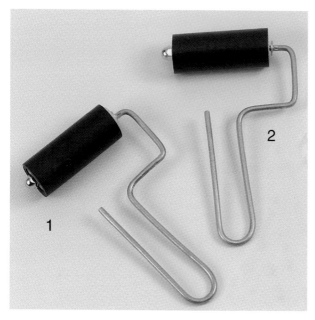

Foam Texturizing Tools

These applicators are useful when a textured or uneven application of adhesive is desired. They also are used when making paste papers.

1. Shoe polish dauber
2. Scratch Art *Lolli-Foam Brush*
3. Scratch Art *Economy Foam Brayer*
4. Darice *Sea Sponges*
5. Plaid *Petifors*
6. Wedge-shaped make-up applicators (purchase these by the bag at drug and variety stores)
7. Darice *Embossing Essentials Foam Daubers* in two sizes

Textures and Patterns

These tools create more of a texture, dimension, or pattern than sponge and foam applicators when applying adhesives and when making paste papers.

1. Scratch Art *Texture Plates*
2. Plaid *Chamois Tool*
3. Plaid *Mopping Tool*
4. Shower puff
5. Copper pan scrubber with handle
6. USArt Quest *Textured Sponge*
7. Plaid *Striated Wall Combs*

Long Handled Tweezers and Hemostats

Use these items to quickly and easily pick up, hold, and position items.

1. Delta *Hold-It*
2. Hemostat (from Clotilde)
3. Dritz *Hold and Release Tweezers*
4. Dritz Tweezers

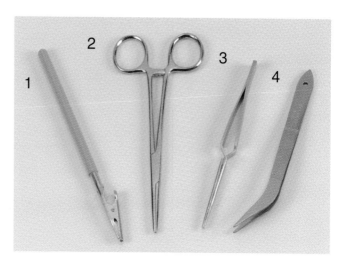

Marking and Scoring Devices

1. Clover Needlecraft, Inc. *Chaco-Liner*: Tiny teeth score multi-layered paper for easy folding
2. Clover Needlecraft, Inc. *Tracing Wheel - Serrated Edges*: Use to cut a saw-tooth edge on paper
3. Clover Needlecraft, Inc. *Tracing Wheel - Blunt Edges*: Use to score light-weight papers
4 and 5. Clover Needlecraft, Inc. *Straight Tailor's Awl* and *Tapered Tailor's Awl*: Sturdy point allows for punching very small holes in heavier surfaces, including mat board, foam core, light-weight plastics, light-weight metal sheets, etc.
6. Clover Needlecraft, Inc. *"Hera" Marker*: Use to score papers and as burnishing tool
7. Clover Needlecraft, Inc. *Finger Presser*: Use to apply adhesives and as burnishing tool
8. *Air Erasable Marker Pen* from Clotilde: Suitable for non-porous surfaces; test prior to use

Measuring Aids

Dritz *Pressure Sensitive Tape Measure* (1) and *Tiger Tape* from Clotilde (2). *Tiger Tape*, a pressure sensitive tape, is available in three marking measurements allowing for accurate placement of items on surfaces. Three Dritz plastic rulers: two *Quilter's Rulers* (3 and 4), one having a metal edge for use with either a craft knife or a rotary cutter, and a wide ruler for use with a rotary cutter (5).

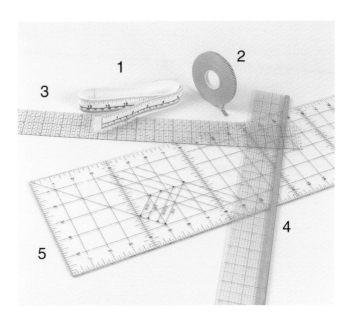

Scissors

1. Olfa *Multi-Purpose Home Scissors, Model SCS-2*: Suitable for several surfaces, including fabric, paper, mat board, cardboard, and light-weight metal
2, 3, and 4. Fiskars *Decorative Edgers*: Suitable for paper; available in a variety of designs
5. Olfa *Olo Rolling Scissors*: Rolling action quickly cuts paper into strips and pieces
6. Back Street, Inc. *Decoupage Scissors*: Suitable for cutting small and/or intricate designs and shapes from paper (decoupage and collage) and fabric (appliqué)

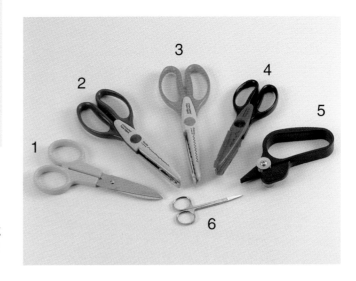

Cutting Tools

From Olfa:
1. *Circular Cutter*
2. *Craft Knife*
3. *Craft Knife* (heavy-duty with snap blades)
4. *Craft Knife* (with snap blades)
5. *Top Sheet Cutter*

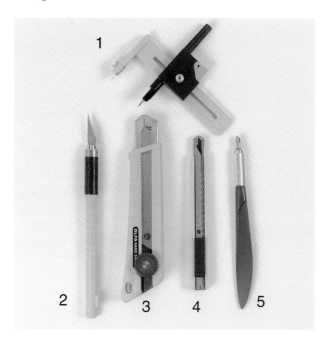

Rotary Cutter Handles, Blades, and Mats

Don't limit the use of a rotary cutter to fabric; it can be used to accurately and quickly cut a wide variety of items, such as paper, card stock, mat board, foam board, cardboard, shrink plastic, craft foam, uncured polymer clay, *Friendly Plastic,* and any other item the blade will cut through. When the blade becomes nicked, it can be used to cut thin metal sheeting and wire.

Fiskars (1), Dritz (2), and Olfa (3) rotary cutters are shown on the large Olfa Cutting Mat (4). Also seen on the large mat is a Dritz Cutting Mat in a smaller size (6) and a Come Quilt With

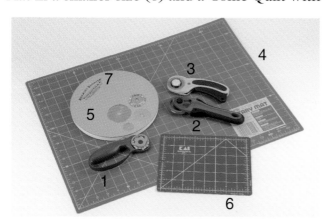

Me *Brooklyn Revolver* (5). Two blades (7) on are the *Brooklyn Revolver.*

In addition to use as a cutting mat, the turntable feature offered by both sizes (only one is shown) of the *Brooklyn Revolver* make this tool a handy and easy-to-use work surface. Protect the surface of the mat with either plastic food wrap or a plastic shower cap when using adhesives, paints, and markers.

Specialized Equipment

1. Clover Needlecraft, Inc. *Craft Iron:* The absence of steam vents is only one bonus offered by this iron
2. Surebonder/FPC Heat Gun
3. Darice Heat Gun

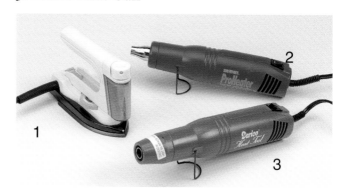

Miscellaneous Helpers

1. Paper Adventures *Lil' Boss*
2. Clover Needlecraft, Inc. *Clamp and Bird Set*
3. June Tailor *Templates for Quilters*

Although very different in usage, each of these tools provides fast and easy methods for crafting techniques. A variety of pressure embossed designs are quickly accomplished in either paper or thin metal sheeting with *The Lil Boss*, cords of twisted ribbon or fibers are easily made when using a *Clamp and Bird Set*, and *Templates for Quilters* are available in several shapes and sizes and are excellent tracing templates for all surfaces.

Chapter 2

Natural Adhesives

No one is exactly certain when the first adhesives were used, but it is known that pastes and glues have been used for more than 4,000 years. Pastes made from a variety of plant starches and fibers were used with papers, while glues made from cheese or the skins, horns, and bones of animals were used with wood. Egg white was the adhesive used for gold leaf in illuminated manuscripts. Casein, a milk protein, was sometimes used as an adhesive, but more often was used as a binder for dry pigments, creating paint. The

manufacturing processes used to produce natural adhesives has changed drastically through the centuries, but these adhesives are still valued and used today.

Gum Arabic

Gum arabic is made from the gum of acacia trees. Its use as an adhesive is limited (it can be used only on porous surfaces, and it is highly sensitive to moisture), but it is widely used as a binder with pigments to create watercolors.

It is available in premixed and powder forms. The powder mixes instantly in water (distilled is recommended), and the viscosity is determined by the ratio of water to powder. Dry pigments, powdered mica pigments, Createx Colors *Pure Pigments* (liquid), and rubber stamping reinkers (with the exception of those that are solvent-based) are added to liquid gum arabic in the amount needed to obtain the desired color. Colored gum arabic can be applied with a foam dauber, brush, USArtQuest *Texture Sponge*, or a rubber brayer. Mix that dries on a palette can be with rejuvenated with a damp brush or a couple drops of water.

If a pigment stamping ink is used to color gum arabic, or if embossing ink is added to colored gum arabic, the solution can be thermal-embossed (refer to Chapter 8). Apply to rubber stamps with either size of Darice *Embossing Essentials Daubers* or a rubber brayer. This mix also can be rejuvenated with a damp brush or water.

Gum arabic applications can be made permanent by applying a spray acrylic finish to the finished project after the gum arabic has dried.

Premixed gum arabic and gum arabic powder are available from U.S. Adhesives; premixed gum arabic is available from Magicalfaerieland (*Faerie Dust*), while gum arabic powder is available from USArtQuest.

The following are coloring agents for natural and synthetic adhesives mentioned throughout the book:

Pigment powders:
- Winsor & Newton
- Twinrocker

Liquid pigments:
- Createx Colors *Pure Pigments*

Powdered mica pigments:
- Magicalfaerieland *Faerie Dust*
- Jacquard Products *Pearl Ex*
- Lemon Tree *Powdered Pearls*
- Twinrocker *Pearlescent Pigments*

Fabric dye powders:
- *Dylon Cold Water Fabric Dye* from Dritz

Water colors:
- Dr. Ph. Martin's *Radiant Concentrated Water Colors*

Permanent inks:
- Dr. Ph. Martin's *Iridescent Calligraphy Colors* and *Bombay India Ink*

Water-based stamping reinkers

Acrylic paints

Arabic Paper

Decorated paper can be used for making envelopes, gift bags, and cards and for embellishing. Adding a double-sided adhesive film to the back of the paper in Step 1 is optional.

> ### You Will Need
> Half sheet Paper Adventures card stock: Teal
> 1 tsp. Magicalfaerieland *Premixed Gum Arabic*
> 1/8 tsp. Magicalfaerieland *Faerie Dust*: Rich Gold
> Rubber stamp (Spiral 1, ©Clearsnap used in sample)
> 1" bristle brush
> Plaid *Patricia Nimocks Clear Acrylic Sealer*
> Miscellaneous supplies: small container with cover for mixing, measuring spoons, craft stick, freezer paper, paper towels
> Optional: Grafix *Double tack,* iron, ironing board, white tissue paper

1. (Optional) If the finished paper will be used to embellish another surface paper, apply double-sided adhesive film to the back of the card stock.
2. Use the craft stick to blend the Rich Gold *Faerie Dust* with the gum arabic in the small container. Stir until smooth. The mixture should brush easily; if necessary, add a drop or two of water.
3. Cut a piece of freezer paper that is at least 2 inches longer and wider than the piece of card stock. Place the card stock on the freezer paper. Brush the colored gum arabic over the surface of the card stock.
4. Stamp on the card stock once, then stamp on a paper towel to clean the colored gum arabic from the stamp. The dry stamp will pick up the colored gum arabic from the surface of the card stock and produce a print of the stamp. Continue stamping and cleaning the stamp each time until the card stock is covered with prints. Allow to dry flat.
5. If the card stock is not flat when dry, place it between two layers of white tissue paper and press flat with an iron set at medium heat. Allow to cool.
6. Spray a light coat of *Clear Acrylic Sealer* over the paper.

Note: If the card stock is to be cut into pieces, do not remove the release paper from the adhesive until all cutting is completed. The edges of the example were cut with a Fiskars *Paper Edger.*

Mucilage

Mucilage is made from one of the following: gum arabic, potato starch, or fish glue. Glycerin is usually added for flex. Primarily used on paper, it forms a weak, water-reversible bond that dries quickly. A thin application rarely wrinkles paper. Results often are better if mucilage is brushed on, rather than if applied from the rubber cap on the bottle. Susceptible to humidity and temperature, mucilage is not a good choice for items that will receive heavy use, frequent handling, or intended for long-term use or display. Mucilage may become quite brittle and discolor over time.

In addition to bonding, mucilage is also used to crackle and craze surfaces painted with acrylic paint; the application of an acrylic finish to the finished project is recommended. To crackle acrylic paint, brush mucilage over dried acrylic paint that has been applied to a surface. Immediately brush another color of acrylic paint over the mucilage. The second coat of acrylic paint will crackle and craze as it dries.

> **Brands of mucilage include:**
> - **Elmer's**
> - **LePages, Inc.**
> - **Ross**

Paste

Paste is made from either plant starch or fibers and is water-reversible. The viscosity determines tack and drying time. The bond ranges from light (rice starch) to moderately heavy (corn and wheat starch). Methyl cellulose and cellulose pastes are fiber-based and are best used on paper that will tolerate a paste with a high water content. High humidity and very cold temperatures may affect the long-term stability of paste. Keep pasted items in a stable environment, out of direct sunlight. In addition to use as an adhesive for porous surfaces, paste also is used for making paper maché, paste paper, and as a binder for dry pigments.

To avoid contaminating the contents of a jar, don't dip tools into a jar of paste as you're working. If you've had problems with paste molding in the jar, it is most likely due to contaminates. Use a clean spoon or craft stick to scoop out the amount needed and place it on a disposable surface (like a paper plate or a piece of paper).

Replace the lid on the jar immediately after use. Tom Terry, of U.S. Adhesives, suggests placing a piece of plastic food wrap over the paste in the jar and pressing it firmly to the paste before replacing the lid. The plastic will reduce water evaporation.

Because paste is usually in a large-mouth jar, it sometimes is difficult twisting the lid off. Placing a second piece of plastic food wrap over the top of the open jar before replacing the lid will prevent the paste from bonding the lid and jar together. (This tip is not limited to paste jars—use it for all of those pesky jars you struggle with opening.)

Should paste begin to dry in the jar, a small amount of water can be blended into it; however, the diluted paste may not have as much tack or bond, and the additional water may cause paper to wrinkle.

Paste that is hard and completely dried out in the jar can be recycled for paper maché, paste paper, and as a binder for dry pigments. Cover the paste with water, replace the lid on the jar, and let sit for 24 hours. Mix well before using (a small whip removes lumps quickly). If the paste is too thin, leave the cover off of the jar for an hour or so to thicken it.

Application

When used for bonding, paste should be applied in a very thin coat—less is best! A thick coat of paste will dry crusty and crinkle and crackle. Too much paste was applied when a dry paste project sounds like a bowl of cereal.

Work on a stack of clean newsprint (Bemiss-Jason has both tablets and packaged sheets) or a phone book. If using a phone book, test the ink's colorfastness by rubbing it with a wet cotton swab; if the ink bleeds or runs, do not use the book. When the paper or page gets covered with paste, discard it.

The best paste applicators have a flat edge, like a craft stick, charge card, small piece of mat board, B & B Etching Products, Inc. etchall *squeegee*, or the Clover Needlecraft, Inc. *Finger Presser*. Depending on the size of the item and/or intended use of the project, paste is applied either to the edges or to the entire surface. If applied only to the edges, apply in a thin coat with the edge of the applicator. If applied to the entire surface, place a small amount of paste in the center of the item. Use the edge of the applicator to pull the paste from the center beyond the edges. If more paste is needed, add only small amounts. In either case, after applying the paste, hold the applicator so that the edge is perpendicular to the surface and gently pull the paste to the outer edges to remove excess. When the paste is in an even, smooth, thin coat, pick up the piece and position it on the surface to which it is being bonded.

Burnishing

Burnishing is highly recommended; it not only smooths the top surface flat, but it also secures the bond. Any of the previously mentioned applicators can be used for burnishing, in addition to a Scratch-Art *Rubbing Stick*, *Hard Rubber Brayer*, or *Soft Rubber Brayer*.

To avoid tearing or marking a surface as it's being burnished, cover it with cooking parchment paper or vellum. After burnishing, remove the covering. If any paste has seeped out from the edges, wipe it off with either a damp cotton swab or blot it up with white tissue paper. Replace the covering, making sure the side that is down is paste-free; burnish again, particularly along the edges. Remove the covering and allow the paste to dry.

Weighting Down

When paste has been applied over a large area, or if the item will receive heavy handling, remove the covering used during burnishing and replace with a clean piece of cooking parchment paper. If the item will not be affected by the weight, place one or two heavy books on top of the parchment paper; otherwise use *Olfa Mini-Weights*, which are small and can be placed directly over pasted areas (with the points up) when the item has raised or textured areas. Leave the books or weights on top of the pasted item overnight.

Storage

Store paste in tightly closed containers, out of direct sunlight, and away from heat and cold. Properly stored premixed and uncooked paste has a shelf life of approximately one year. Cooked paste has a very short shelf life, so prepare only the amount you will use within two days.

Starch and Fiber Pastes

Starch and fiber pastes are available in premixed and powder forms. Some dry forms require cooking, while some are simply mixed with water (distilled is recommended). Gane Bros. & Lane *Yes! Paste* (corn-based) is in premixed form. University Products *Wheat Paste* is cooked in the microwave, *Belgian Rice Starch* requires cooking on the stove, and *Zen Instant Wheat Paste* (also available in premixed form) and *Methyl Cellulose Paste* do not require cooking and mix in water (distilled is recommended). Twinrocker *Methyl Cellulose* and Ross *Art Paste* (a cellulose paste) mix easily in water; in addition to the uses mentioned for paste, these products also can be used as marbling size.

Instructions for blending small amounts of Ross *Art Paste* are found on page 21; instructions for Twinrocker *Methyl Cellulose* are found on page 22.

Products labeled "school paste" should not be expected to perform to the level, or have the longevity, provided by higher quality pastes; however, they can be diluted and used for paste paper, paper maché, and as a binder for dry pigments.

Wallpaper paste is available in premixed and powder forms. The most common craft uses for these products are paper maché or paste paper. When mixing and using powdered wallpaper paste, it is advisable to wear plastic gloves; most brands contain fungicides and insecticides that may be hazardous to your health.

Bemiss-Jason *MagiCraft Shred, Sheets*, and *Tape* are impregnated with a starch paste; a quick dip in water activates it. Available in several colors, the products are quick and easy to use when creating decorative items, including those of paper maché.

Project

Collage Greeting Card

Designed by Sue Giduck

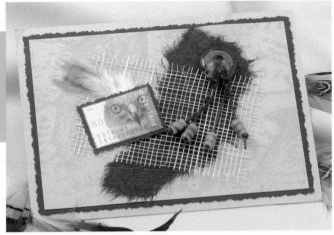

This is a beautiful example of a card using a combination of items to create a collage. If unable to locate the items used in this card, substitute with those of your choice. Handwrite your greeting on the back and include an adhesive easel back in the envelope, so the card can be displayed upon receipt.

You Will Need:

4-1/2- x 6-inch piece of card stock (color of your choice)

4-1/4- x 5-3/4-inch piece of cover-weight paper or origami paper (color of your choice)

3- x 5-1/2-inch piece of card stock (can be same color or pattern as larger piece)

Assorted items for collage: example has faux postage stamp mounted on black cover-weight paper, feather, torn black mulberry paper, piece of natural abacca ribbon, glass bead with a center hole, three polymer clay beads on black beading cord

Yes! Paste

Aleene's *Jewel Glue*

Deckle-cut scissors

Craft knife, paper cutter, or rotary cutter and mat

Scrap vellum or cooking parchment paper to use when burnishing

Art Accents *Stick-On Easel Back*

Miscellaneous supplies: ruler, applicator for paste, burnishing tool

---

1. Cut all papers to needed sizes, using the deckle-cut scissors to cut the black paper. Bond the black paper to the larger piece of card stock with the paste. Cover with the vellum (or parchment paper) and burnish in place. Remove the vellum. Bond the smaller piece of card stock to the black paper with paste. Cover with the vellum and burnish in place. Apply a small amount of the paste to the center back of the torn mulberry paper. Position it on the card stock and burnish gently with the tips of your fingers. Set aside.

2. Bond the faux postage stamp to the black paper with the paste; burnish with your fingertips. Using the deckle-cut scissors, trim the black paper close to the edges of the postage stamp. Using a small amount of the paste, bond the feather to the back of the black paper. Set aside.

3. Add the polymer beads on the cording to the round glass jewel. Apply a light coating of the paste to the center area of the abacca ribbon and bond it to the torn mulberry paper. Burnish in place with your fingertips.

4. Using *Jewel Glue*, bond the glass bead to the torn mulberry paper, overlapping the abacca ribbon at the top. Bond the faux postage stamp to the abacca ribbon; the application of paste should be enough to bond the abacca ribbon to the card stock. Allow to dry.

Paste Paper

Paste paper is easy to make. Best of all, the results are an inexpensive decorated paper that can be used in a variety of ways in paper crafts. There's no such thing as a bad sheet of paste paper. What didn't look appealing when first done often takes on a new life when cut into strips, squares, and circles, or used in paper punches. Save all of the bits and pieces—you'll be amazed how often that stash will provide the perfect finishing touch for a project!

Just about every type of paper can be used when making paste paper. Sketch paper, watercolor paper (either cold or hot pressed), kraft paper (either white or colored), paper grocery bags, and card stock are a few to consider. Mat board tends to separate, but can be used, high-gloss papers present problems (the paste may lift from the surface), and tissue paper is better suited for pasted paper (see page 23).

When preparing to make paste paper, cover the work area with several thicknesses of newspaper, which will help keep clean-up chores to a minimum. Place either a piece of freezer paper, shiny side up, or a sheet of 6mm Darice *Foamies* (a craft foam) on the newspapers. Either will be the work surface for the paste paper and should be larger than the sheet of paper being used.

Although it's not required to dampen the paper and allow it to dry before beginning, the time required is short, and it often improves the finished results. Wetting the paper shrinks and relaxes its fibers. In some cases, it removes sizing that was added during the manufacturing process. If using a colored paper, you'll know in an instant if the paper is colorfast. Paper that is not colorfast can be used; however, the color will bleed and affect the colors that are added to the paste. **Note:** Do not dampen mat board before beginning, because it will separate.

Dip the sheet of paper into water or hold it under a running faucet. Shake off the excess water, place the sheet on the work surface, and smooth flat. Blot excess water from the top of the sheet with paper towels. Allow to dry. If the sheet is wrinkled and bowed when dry, place it between two layers of white tissue paper and press flat with an iron on medium heat. Place the flat sheet on the work surface and apply the colored paste as directed below.

Another method is to brush water over the back of the sheet. Turn the paper over, place it on the work surface, and smooth flat. Brush water over the front of the sheet and blot the excess from the sheet with paper towels. Apply the colored paste as directed below.

If the sheet was not dampened, place it on the work surface and apply the colored paste as directed below.

Use clean containers with tight fitting lids when mixing and for storage of the mixed paste solution. With the exception of pastes that are cooked and wallpaper paste powder, the mixed solution will have a shelf life of several months if stored correctly.

Dilute premixed paste with a small amount of water (distilled is recommended); the consistency should be about that of thick sour cream. Using distilled water, mix paste powder as directed on the box; if necessary, dilute to the aforementioned consistency. **Note:** To make a smaller amount of Ross *Art Paste*, blend 2 tablespoons of the powder with 3/4 cups of water; cover and let sit covered for two hours. Stir again before using (no further stirring will be needed).

Twinrocker Methyl Cellulose

To mix Twinrocker Methyl Cellulose, mix one teaspoon powder to one cup of water; for larger amounts, use one tablespoon powder to three cups of water. Add the water to a container having a tight fitting lid. Sprinkle the powder over the water in as even a layer as possible. Cover the container and allow to sit for 24 hours. Remove the lid and gently stir the paste until smooth. The paste may require being stirred each time it is used. Store covered in the mixing container.

> **To make colored paste to use for paste paper, place the needed amount of the paste in a container. Usually three to four tablespoons of paste will be adequate for an 8-1/2- x 11-inch sheet of paper. Add the selected coloring agent (see page 16) in the amount necessary to reach the desired color; stir until well blended. Store in a tightly covered container out of direct sunlight.**

A diluted paste solution should be smooth and free of lumps; blend well with a plastic fork or small whip. If the paste is too thin, leave the cover off the container for an hour or so before using.

Applying a double-sided adhesive film that can be thermal embossed (refer to Chapter 7) to the back of the paper before beginning is optional. In some cases, having the film in place is very handy. The release paper on the back of the film also helps keep the sheet of paper flat. If pressing is necessary, it will not affect the adhesive feature of this type of film.

A variety of tools can be used to apply the colored paste to the paper, including inexpensive bristle paintbrushes, any of the foam applicators shown in Chapter 1 (see page 13), a rubber spatula, Scratch Art *Rubber Brayer* (hard or soft) and *Rubbing Stick*, or Royal Brush MFG Co. *Squeeze and Flo Brush*.

Apply enough paste to cover the paper. The paste should be brushed beyond the edges of the sheet onto the work surface. This will hold the paper in place and keep it flat.

Create patterns, textures, and designs using one of the applicator tools, foam stamps, pieces of sponge, sponge stamps, pieces of craft foam that have been cut with a decorative paper edger, shower puffs, pan scrubbers (those with a handle on the back are the easiest to use), USArtQuest *Texture Sponge*, Plaid *Chamois Tool, Striated Wall Comb,* and *Mopping Tool* (see page 13).

If the paste doesn't hold the design made by the tool, either too much paste was applied to the paper or the paste is too thin. Remove excess paste with an applicator tool; Faux Paste Paper (refer to Chapter 3) is better suited when a heavy application of paste is desired. If the paste is too thin, wait a few minutes for the paste to thicken on the paper.

Multiple colors of paste can be used to create swirled effects, and a small paintbrush can be used to marble multiple colors. Allow one color of paste to dry, cover with a stencil, and apply a second color over the stencil; lift the stencil after the paste has begun to set.

Embellishments such as powdered mica pigments, glitter, Signature Crafts *Glitter Slivers*, small pieces of colored papers (torn, cut, or punched), dried flowers, dried leaves, ribbon, and fibers can be added before the paste has begun to set. Sprinkle the pigments and glitter over the wet glue; press the larger items into the wet glue with the tip of a wooden skewer.

Leave the paper on the work surface until the paste feels dry; a hair dryer can be used to hasten drying. If freezer paper was used, gently lift the sheet from it; if placed on 6 mm Darice *Foamies,* bend the *Foamies* into an upside down "U," and the sheet will pop off. Discard the freezer paper, or rinse the *Foamies* under running water to remove the colored paste. Place the paste paper sheet on a cake cooling rack or piece of screening and allow to dry.

If the paper is wrinkled and/or bowed when dry, place it, paste side down, on two sheets of white tissue paper. Cover the back with two sheets of white tissue paper; press the paper flat with an iron set at medium heat (use a lower heat if glitter was applied to the paste).

Several of the self-adhesive embellishing products mentioned in Chapter 7 can be added after the paste has dried and the paper has been pressed.

Paste paper does not have a permanent surface. An acrylic medium can be mixed with the paste to make it permanent; usually the proportion of paste to acrylic medium is three parts paste to one part acrylic medium, although those proportions can be altered. A spray acrylic finish applied after the paste has dried also will make the surface permanent.

Technique

Pasted Paper

Pasted paper is made with uncolored paste; the tissue paper is not colorfast and provides the color. The finished paper can be used in a variety of ways, including a background paper for stamped projects torn, cut, or punched embellishments on paper projects, or covers for handmade books. When a permanent surface is necessary, apply a spray acrylic finish to the paper after it has dried.

You Will Need
Uncolored paste as prepared for Paste Paper (see pages 20 and 21)
Piece of freezer paper, larger and wider than the tissue
Scissors
1-inch wide foam brush, Scratch-Art *Lolli-Foam Brush*, or Royal Brush MFG Co. *Brush & Flow*
Two to four colors of Bemiss-Jason *Spectra Tissue*, one sheet of each color
Heat gun or hair dryer

1. Cut each sheet of tissue into quarters.
2. Place the freezer paper shiny side up on a flat surface. Place two cut pieces of tissue in the center of the freezer paper; if using multiple colors, begin with the darkest.
3. Brush the paste over the edges of the tissue to anchor it to the freezer paper; working from the center out, brush paste over the tissue's surface. The tissue does not have to be smooth and flat. If the paste is difficult to brush, dipping just the end of the brush in water will make brushing easier.
4. Cover with another piece of tissue (either the same color or lighter). Brush paste over this layer. Repeat so there are four layers of tissue.
5. Allow to dry; a heat gun or hair dryer can be used to hasten drying. Remove from the freezer paper. If applying a spray acrylic finish (optional), do this before removing the sheet from the freezer paper.

- The tissue pieces do not need to all be the same size; torn and scrap pieces of tissue can be used.
- For a heavier paper, use more than four layers.
- Crumple the tissue to create texture and dimension.
- Pleat the tissue using Clotilde's *Perfect Pleater*. Each layer can be placed with the pleats going in different directions, or unpleated and pleated layers can be alternated.
- Narrow ribbon, small dried flowers, Art Institute Glitter, Bemiss-Jason Glitter, and powdered mica pigments (see page 16) are some of the items that can be placed on the top layer while the paste is still wet.
- You can use white tissue paper for the first three layers and then place small colored prints, Signature Crafts *Glitter Silvers*, Magicalfaerieland *Faerie Glass*, Yasutomo Mizuhiki Cord, or powdered mica pigments on the third layer; cover with a layer of white tissue and apply paste. When pasted, the top layer of tissue will secure these items in place.
- Use this technique for making small paper maché projects: Rather than freezer paper as a work surface, place the paper on or in some type of mold. A minimum of six layers of tissue is recommended. (See below for more information).

Technique

Paper Maché

The traditional method of making paper maché uses torn paper strips (sometimes pieces) that are coated with a paste solution after being placed over some type of mold. At one time, newspapers were the common paper supply, but today, newsprint is preferred because the newspaper ink usually is not permanent; as the paste is applied, the paper becomes grungy looking. With newsprint, the bleeding ink problem is eliminated by purchasing either a roll end of newsprint from the local newspaper or packaged cut sheets from the craft store (Bemiss-Jason is one brand available in precut sheets). Other papers to consider include pages from phone books (provided the ink is permanent), grocery bags, kraft

paper, and tissue paper. The only requirements are that the paper readily absorbs the paste and is easy to tear into strips.

Tear the paper to feather the edge; feathered edges absorb more paste, making them more pliable and less visible when dry. The sizes of the torn pieces are determined by the size of the finished object: a small box would not use strips as long or as wide as a large bowl.

Paste used in making paper maché is generally diluted with water. The paste solution should be thin enough to be absorbed by the paper but thick enough to bond the strips together. Heavier papers (grocery bags or kraft papers) can be soaked in the solution briefly to ensure that the paper has absorbed the paste. The solution is applied either by brush or hand to thinner papers as they are placed on the mold.

Molds can be made from non-hardening children's clay or moldable metal mesh when a specific shape is desired. Any stable form that is not affected by moisture also can be used, including metal, china, glass, or plastic items. The mold is either sprayed or coated with a finish the paste will not adhere to (for example *Silicone*), or covered with plastic cooking wrap.

After preparing the mold, place one strip on the mold beginning in the center, then slightly overlap it with a second strip. Apply the paste solution over the second strip. Place a third strip on the second; the edge of the third should slightly overlap the edge of the second; apply paste over the third strip. Continue in this manner until the entire surface of the mold is covered with pasted strips. If the amount of paste is excessive, blot with paper towels.

Begin another layer of strips, this time placing them across (perpendicular to) the first layer. Usually, little paste is needed for this layer. Use either your fingers or a brush to secure and smooth the second layer on the first; apply only enough paste necessary for a secure bond, and blot any excess.

The number of layers necessary depends upon the end use of the project and the type of paper used. An item that will receive heavy handling will require more layers then a deco-rative item; kraft paper will require fewer layers than newsprint.

High humidity greatly affects drying time. A fan, hair dryer, or heat gun can be used to partially dry a layer before another is added. Too many wet layers can result in moldy paper maché. If this happens, start over!

When all layers have been added, place the project on a cake drying rack or a piece of screening, if possible, in front of an open window or fan. Leave the project on the mold until the paste feels dry; the sides of the project should be firm and stable. Gently remove it from the mold and allow to dry completely. Projects made using moldable metal mesh as a form can be left on the form until dry. If necessary, use scissors to neaten edges after the paper maché is dry.

Dry paper maché projects can be painted with craft paints and embellished with just about any type of supply desired. An acrylic finish (spray or brush) is optional.

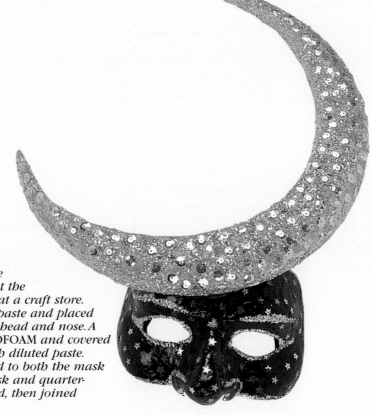

Chris Hansen used paper maché to create this stellar mask. It's hard to imagine that the beginnings were a half mask purchased at a craft store. Strips of paper were coated with diluted paste and placed over the mask to create the extended forehead and nose. A quarter-moon shape was cut from STYROFOAM and covered with strips of paper that were coated with diluted paste. Three layers of paper maché were applied to both the mask and the quarter-moon. When dry, the mask and quarter-moon were painted, glittered, and jeweled, then joined together. Truly spectacular!

Faux Paper Maché

Although a two-section acrylic ornament in the shape of a tree was used in the sample, any two-section acrylic ornament could be used. The other half of the ornament was used for the shaker card seen on page 133.

> ### You Will Need
> One section of a two-section acrylic ornament in the desired shape and size
> White tissue paper
> Green Dr. Ph Martins *Radiant Concentrated Water Color*
> Ross *White Paste*
> Sunday International *Foil Magic Adhesive*
> Gold Sunday International *Craft Foil*
> ColArt Americas *Glass & Tile Colors Base Coat/Top coat Varnish*
> *Silicone* spray
> Miscellaneous tools: Small container for mixing paste, small amount of water, craft stick, small brush

1. Tear the tissue into pieces that are slightly larger than the inside of the ornament. Place six layers of the torn tissue into ornament; the edges of the tissue should extend slightly beyond the outer edges of the ornament. Dampen the brush in water and gently pat it over the tissue so that all layers of the tissue are damp and mold to the inside of the ornament. Allow to dry.

2. Place two teaspoons of the paste in a small container; add the green *Water Color* to reach the desired color. If necessary, add a small amount of water to the colored paste so that it is the

consistency of milk. If this dilutes the color of the paste, add more ink.

3. Spray the outside of the ornament with *Silicone*. Gently remove the formed tissue from the inside of the ornament and place it over the outside of the ornament. Brush the colored paste over the tissue paper; all layers of the tissue should be damp from the colored paste. Allow to dry.

4. Leaving the formed tissue on the outside of the ornament, randomly brush a light coating of *Foil Magic Adhesive* randomly over the surface of the tissue paper. When the adhesive is clear and tacky, apply the dull side of the foil to the adhesive. Lift the clear covering from the foil. Repeat until all areas of the adhesive are covered with the foil.

5. Apply a light coating of the varnish over the formed tissue. When dry, remove the formed tissue from the ornament. Trim away excess tissue from the edges.

Hide and Fish Glues

Hide and fish glues are animal protein-based and water-reversible. For centuries, these glues, which form a strong bond that will withstand heavy use, have been used by furniture and cabinetmakers. The slow set time allows for repositioning of pieces being joined. Hide and fish glues are not recommended for outdoor projects.

Hide glues were available only in flake or powder form until 1935 when Franklin International introduced TiteBond *Liquid Hide Glue*, a ready-to-use hide glue. Although still available in flake and powders, even the most ardent crafter purchases the ready-made liquid product. The process required to make hide glue is a smelly and sticky one—the flakes or powders are softened in water and then cooked to the proper viscosity.

LePages *Original Glue* was the first fish glue available in liquid form. Prior to that, a procedure similar to that of hide glue flakes and powders was necessary. *Original Glue* is water-reversible and can be used on a variety of porous and non-porous surfaces. Depending on the project, clamping may be necessary until the glue has cured.

In addition to their uses as an adhesive, hide and fish glues also can be used for crackling and crazing surfaces painted with flat latex paint.

Rubber Cement

Rubber cement was introduced during the nineteenth century. Made from rubber tree gum, it is the only natural adhesive that is not water-reversible and is solvent-based. It is highly flammable and requires caution during use. Read and follow all manufacturer's directions.

Rubber cement has a great deal of flex, is repositionable, doesn't wrinkle paper, provides a medium bond, and is suitable for several surfaces, including leather. It is easily removed from most surfaces by rubbing with your finger.

Brands of rubber cement include:
- Elmer's
- Ross

Tri-Tix *Rubber Cream Glue* has all of the features of rubber cement and can be used for the same techniques, but it differs from rubber cement in that it is non-toxic and non-flammable.

Chapter 3

All-Purpose
White and Tacky Glues

When polyvinyl acetate (PVA) glue was introduced in the mid-1940s, it was intended as an adhesive for the building trades. This water-based synthetic adhesive was called white glue, not only for its color, but also to differentiate it from brown-colored animal glues. It wasn't long before crafters discovered white glue; through the years, it has been used for just about every crafting activity imaginable!

Aleene introduced *Tacky Glue* in the 1950s as a solution to the problem of white glue leaking through the petals of silk flowers her company was manufacturing. Although the formulas of white and tacky glues are not the same, tacky glue also is a water-based, non-toxic, synthetic adhesive.

As is the case with all liquid adhesives, avoid contaminating the contents of a jar or bottle of these glues (see page 18). Either pour or use a clean plastic spoon or craft stick to scoop out the amount needed onto a disposable, non-stick surface (cooking parchment paper, freezer paper, plastic plate, etc.).

Surfaces involved must be dry and free of oil and dust before applying either white or tacky glue. When applying to surfaces that will be bonded, work on either a stack of clean newsprint or a phone book (test the ink for bleeding; see page 18). Discard the top layer of paper or the page as it becomes covered with glue.

When applying more than one coat of either diluted or full-strength white or tacky glue, it's important to allow each coat to dry completely before adding the next. The glue should be clear without any white streaks. A hair dryer at low heat, held at least 6 inches from the glue, can be used to hasten drying after the glue has begun to set (the color will change from white to clear). If the final coat feels sticky after drying, apply an acrylic finish to the project.

There is nothing in a white or tacky glue that would cause it to discolor slightly over time; however, most brands are not UV-resistant. Those that are UV-resistant will include that information on the label. If the product you have selected does not have that feature, items can be protected from the environment by covering with a UV-resistant surface (i.e. glass, *Mylar*, or acrylic) or by applying a UV-resistant acrylic finish

All-purpose White Glue

This glue can be used on a variety of surfaces. Select a product suitable for the surfaces being used and always test when the surfaces are those not recommended by the manufacturer.

White glue forms a medium bond; it is not intended to support heavy objects. Further, it is not recommended for use on items that will be placed outdoors. The viscosity of most brands is in the medium range. Several types are in squeeze-type bottles, and all are easy to apply. The glue provides a medium tack. Depending upon the brand, flex varies from limited to moderate. Those containing a high water content will set and dry slowly. White glue is clear (some more so than others) when dry.

Before a PVA glue has dried, it is easily removed with water. Although water-reversible when dry, most are not as easily removed as natural adhesives; some may require scrubbing with a strong detergent or household cleaner for complete removal.

Test before beginning a paper project to

determine if the product you have selected will wrinkle it. Those with a thin viscosity may soak through thinner papers and fabrics. Thin papers or fabrics can be sealed with a very light coat of glue applied with either a brush or rubber brayer; do not push the glue into the fibers of the paper or fabric. Allow to dry; apply the amount of glue needed for bonding over the dried glue.

When a thicker viscosity is desired, allow a puddle of the glue to sit on a disposable, non-stick surface; the glue will thicken as the water evaporates. Freezing white glue to thicken it is not recommended by most manufacturers.

Apply only in the amount needed when bonding surfaces; excessive amounts of glue can result in a poor bond. When a fine line of glue is needed, place it in a fine-tipped applicator bottle (as seen on page 11) when the bottle of glue does not have an applicator tip. Most white glues also can be applied with a dampened brush or sponge applicator.

A rubber brayer is an excellent tool to use for applying a thin, even coat of glue over a surface. Pour the needed amount onto a piece of freezer paper, shiny side up; roll the brayer through the glue. If the glue is not evenly distributed over the brayer, roll it one or two times over a clean area of the freezer paper.

White glue can be diluted with water (distilled is recommended). The amount of dilution is determined by the use and the surfaces involved; test before beginning. Diluted glue is used as a glaze (colored and clear), for paper maché, faux paste paper, collage, decoupage, molded embellishments, and as a binder for dry and liquid coloring supplies (see page 16).

White glues (diluted and full-strength) can be colored with a variety of coloring supplies. For a listing of possible coloring agents, see page 16.

Plaid *Soft Flock Adhesive*, packaged with *Soft Flock*, is a colored PVA. In addition to use with *Soft Flock*, the adhesive also can be used for bonding and for making faux paste paper (see page 34). It can be added to the surface of faux paste paper, or used with stamps for flocked prints (stamped images).

Twinrocker *Book Binders Slow Drying Glue* is formulated to set slowly to allow for an extended repositioning time. It can be mixed with Twinrocker *Archival, Neutral pH, Permanent Glue* when a faster set is desired; the greater the proportion of *Archival Glue*, the faster the set. The glue also can be used for making paste paper (see page 21).

Green Sneakers *Lick & Stick*, Jim Stephan *Envelope Glue*, and Twinrocker *Remoistenable Glue* are intended for use on envelope flaps and for making stickers (refer to Chapter 4); however, they also can be used for bonding provided the pieces are joined together immediately after the glue has been applied.

Store white glues (including those that are diluted and/or colored) in a tightly closed container, away from heat and cold, and out of direct sunlight. If properly stored, the glue has a shelf life of up to two years.

Brands of all-purpose white glues include:

- Aabbitt Adhesives, Inc. *Jade*
- Aleene's *All-Purpose White Glue*
- Bond *Stik* and *Instant GRRRIP*
- Books by Hand *PVA*
- Crayola *Art & Craft Glue*
- Delta *Sobo*
- Dr. Ph. Martin's *Glue Everything* (permanent and non-water-reversible)
- Elmer's *Glue-All*
- Franklin International *TiteBond Home and School Glue* and *TiteBond Thick and Quick* (packaged in a pressurized container)
- Gane Brothers & Lane *53S Adhesive*
- Green Sneakers *Lick & Stick*
- Jim Stephan *Envelope Glue*
- Ross *All Purpose White Glue* and *Craft Glue*
- Twinrocker *Archival, Neutral pH, Permanent Glue, Book Binders Slow Drying Glue* (a PVA/methyl cellulose blend), and *Remoistenable Glue*
- UHU *Crafts Glue* (distributed by Saunders)
- University Products *Lineco pH neutral PVA Glue*
- U.S. Adhesives *T-29*

Decorated Boxes

All-purpose white glue blended with coloring supplies provides the textured surface on these boxes.

You Will Need

Paper maché boxes, 2 to 4 inches across by 2 to 4 inches deep
U.S. Adhesives *T-29 Glue*
DecoArt *Dazzling Metallics*: Glorious Gold
DecoArt *Crafter's Acrylics*: Hunter Green
Createx Colors *Pure Pigment*: Pthalo Green
Jacquard Products *Pearl Ex*: Antique Gold
1/2- and 1-inch bristle brushes
Spray acrylic finish
Disposable, non-stick surface
Miscellaneous supplies: craft sticks, emery board, paper towels

For All Boxes

1. Using the 1/2-inch brush, paint the inside, top rim, and underside of the box and the inside of the lid with either Glorious Gold or Hunter Green. Allow to dry. Clean the brush and set aside; use the 1-inch brush for the other steps.

2. For the glue/*Pearl Ex* Antique Gold blend, place a tablespoon-sized puddle of glue on the work surface. Sprinkle approximately 1/4 teaspoon powdered mica pigment over the glue. Blend the color into the glue by dragging the end of a craft stick through the puddle; the glue and the powder do not have to be completely mixed together.

3. For the glue/*Pure Pigment* Pthalo Green blend, place a tablespoon-sized puddle of glue on the work surface. Add two or three drops of the liquid pigment to the top of the glue. Blend the color into the glue by dragging the end of a craft stick through the puddle; the glue and the liquid do not have to be completely mixed together.

Note: Do not apply the glue blend to the rim at the top of the box that is covered by the sides of the lid. A hair dryer can be used to hasten drying of the glue blend between steps.

For the Square Gold Box

1. Brush the glue/Pthalo Green blend to the top and outer edges of the lid and to the sides of the box. Some streaks of glue will be visible. Allow to dry.

2. Brush the glue/Antique Gold blend over the same areas. Some streaks of glue will be visible. Allow to dry.

3. Using the fine side of the emery board, lightly sand the glue/Antique Gold to expose small sections of the glue/Pthalo Green. Wipe off the sanded areas with a slightly damp paper towel. Allow to dry.

4. Apply an acrylic finish to the lid and box.

For the Round Green Boxes

1. Brush a heavy coat of the glue/Pthalo Green blend over the top and outer edges of the lid and the sides of the box. Allow to dry.
2. Brush the glue/Antique Gold blend over portions of the green on the bottom of the box; brush the same color over the entire top of the lid. Allow to dry. Set the bottom of the box aside.
3. Using the side of the brush, pat the glue/Pthalo blend over the top of the lid. When the blend has almost set, drag the tip of the brush through the blend, exposing the glue/Antique Gold blend. Allow to dry.
4. Apply an acrylic finish to the lid and box.

For the Oval Green Box

1. Allow the glue/Antique Gold blend to sit uncovered until the blend begins to thicken; do not allow the blend to set. This will take approximately 30 minutes in areas where humidity is low to one hour in areas where humidity is high.
2. Brush a heavy coat of the glue/Antique Gold blend over the top and sides of the lid and the sides of the box. Allow to dry.
3. Allow the glue/Pthalo Green blend to sit uncovered until the blend begins to thicken; do not allow the blend to set (this will take 15 to 30 minutes).
4. Fold one piece of paper towel into quarters. Tap the folded edge on the glue/Pthalo Green blend. Pat the folded edge on the lid and sides of the box, adding more of the blend to the towel as necessary. Continue applying the blend in this manner until the desired texture is reached. Allow to dry.
5. Apply an acrylic finish to the lid and box.

School Glues

School glues are water-based, non-toxic, and polyvinyl-based. They are formulated to be easily removed from surfaces after drying. As a result, they are more susceptible to moisture than all-purpose white glue, so apply an acrylic finish to projects intended for long-term use. School glues have many of the features of all-purpose white glue, but depending on the brand, the bond and tack may not be as strong and some dry quite brittle with little flex.

Elmer's *GluColors* and Ross *Playtime Glue* are two brands of school glue available in colors. White school glue can be colored with the same supplies used for all-purpose white glues, in addition to poster paints (dry and premixed) (see page 16).

Brands of white school glue include:
- Aleene's *Budget School Glue*
- Beacon Adhesives *Kids Choice Glue*
- Elmer's *School Glue*
- Leech Products, Inc. *Tap-N-Glue*
- Ross *School Glue* and *White Glue*

Tacky Glues

Tacky glues can be used on a variety of porous, semi-porous, and non-porous surfaces. When using surfaces not mentioned on the label of the product you have selected, test before beginning, but keep in mind that none are suitable for use on items that will be exposed to the elements.

As the name implies, tacky glues provide a high degree of tack; securing adjoining pieces while the glue sets often is not necessary. Most are very thick: they stay where applied and rarely drip. They dry clear (some more than others), and the viscosity varies somewhat between brands, but all are thicker than all-purpose white glues. Most brands can be frozen when an even thicker viscosity is desired.

Tacky glues are easily removed from surfaces before they have dried. Although water-reversible, some may require soaking and then scrubbing with a heavy detergent or household cleaner to be completely removed when dry.

The method of application and the tools used are determined by the surface involved and the project. When bonding, do not apply excessive amounts. When applied over an area, follow the directions in Chapter 2 for applying paste and use the same tools. Bands or drops of glue can be applied either with Aleene's *Tacky Glue Syringe* or from an applicator bottle; it may be necessary to clip off the end of a plastic tip to enable the glue to flow from it.

Thin-bodied tacky glues provide the same tack and can be used in the same techniques as the thicker ones, although these thinner glues are easier to apply and better suited for certain techniques. You can apply them either from the bottle tip, with a rubber brayer, or a dampened brush, and most can be applied with a fine-tipped applicator (as seen on page 11).

Both types of tacky glue can be diluted and used in the same ways as diluted white glue (see page 29); coloring supplies mentioned for white glue also are suitable for these glues.

> **Brands of tacky glues include:**
> - Activa *Mighty Tacky*
> - Aleene's *Original Tacky Glue*, *Thick Designer Tacky Glue*, and *Tacky Thin-Bodied Glue*
> - Bond *Squeezable Tacky* and *484: Tacky*
> - Crafter's Pick *Incredibly Tacky*
> - Delta *Velverette* and *Quik 'n Tacky*

Paper Sculpture, designed by Jill Meyer. Jill created this stunning design using sketch paper. Each section was cut out from sketch paper, then scored and either creased or folded to create dimension. The pieces were layered on foam core. Aleene's Thin Bodied Tacky Glue was used to bond together the many layers necessary for the intricate design. To protect the piece, a UV-resistant glass covers the frame. Jill is a frequent contributor to stamping magazines, and she also designs stamps for several companies.

Aabbitt Adhesives, Inc. *Super 88* and Crafter's Pick *"The Ultimate"* are similar to a tacky glue; however, each offers properties not found in all tacky glues. *The Ultimate* can be used as a contact glue on many surfaces, including polymer clay and metal. To use as a contact glue, apply a thin layer of glue to each surface. Allow to dry until almost clear; some streaks of white will be visible. Position the two surfaces together and use finger pressure to hold smaller surfaces together until the bond is secure (this occurs within a few moments). Larger items should be secured together until the glue is completely dry. *Super 88* is very thick. It is especially good for bonding large pieces of hard plastic foam together and to other surfaces. This product often is used by theater set designers due to the strong bond it forms. It is not recommended for use by children.

Store tacky glue products (including those that have been diluted and/or colored) in tightly closed containers, out of direct sunlight, and away from heat and cold. If properly stored, the shelf life for most products is approximately two years.

Project

Green Patina Maple Leaf Box

Designed by American Traditional Stencils

The combination of tacky glue and copper paint create the faux metal leaves that decorate this box. The results are very realistic!

You Will Need

American Traditional Stencil *BLT-337 Maple Leaf*
Paper maché box
Beacon *Kid's Choice Glue*
DecoArt *Patio Paint*: Honest Copper
Aleene's *Enhancer's Matte Varnish*
Duncan *Aged Metal Patina*: Green
Empty paint or glue bottle with a fine tip
Flat 1/2-inch artist paintbrush
Miscellaneous supplies: Masking tape, pencil, soft cloth

1. Using the tape to hold the stencil in place, randomly trace the maple leaf onto the top and sides of the box. The tracings can overlap, if desired.
2. Place the glue in the fine-tipped bottle; outline the leaf shapes with glue. Allow to dry.
3. Fill in the outlined leaf shapes with more glue until they are completely covered. Allow to dry.
4. Using the brush, apply a coat of copper paint to the entire box. Allow to dry. Repeat several times.
5. Apply the varnish to the entire box. Allow to dry.
6. Antique the box by applying the green paint over all surfaces, concentrating it in the veins and around the outer edges of the leaves. Wipe off excess as necessary the soft cloth. Allow to dry.

Basic Paper Maché

Follow the paper maché instructions in Chapter 2, substituting either a white or tacky glue for the paste. Dilute the glue so that it is readily absorbed by the selected paper, but test before starting. The glue on one layer of paper strips should be clear (dry) before adding another layer of paper strips. If the project feels sticky after all of the glue has dried, apply an acrylic finish.

Project

Faux Paper Maché

This is somewhat of a departure from traditional paper maché. Absolutely and completely faux paper maché probably is a more accurate name.

You Will Need

Activa *Rigid Wrap*

Activa *Mighty Tacky*

One sheet Bemiss-Jason *Fadeless Tissue*: Red

Craf-t Products *Metallic Rub-Ons*: Gold

Plaid *Petifors*

Delta *Renaissance Foil Easy Crackle System**: *Gold Crackle Kit* (supplies can be purchased separately, if desired)

1-inch Royal Brush MFG Co. brush

Miscellaneous supplies: bowl for use as form (approximately 6-inch diameter), sponge, plastic food wrap, tape measure, small container with cover, craft sticks, scissors

*Due to the texture of *Rigid Wrap*, the use of *Renaissance Foil Crackle Medium* included in the kit is optional; it was not used in the sample.

1. Wipe the outside of the bowl with a damp sponge. Cover the outside of the bowl with plastic food wrap; smooth the plastic over the bowl so that it is wrinkle free.

2. Going from side to side, measure the length across the outside of the bowl; add 2 inches to that measurement. Cut four strips of *Rigid Wrap* that length. Dampen the *Rigid Wrap* as directed on the package. Referring to the photos, place two strips across the bowl, and then two more strips in the opposite direction. The surface of the plastic bowl should be completely covered with *Rigid Wrap*; cut and add more strips, if necessary. When all strips are in place, smooth flat. Allow to dry. Apply a second layer of strips in the same manner after the first has dried. Allow to dry.

3. Dilute the *Might Tacky* with an equal amount of water in the small container; blend well with a craft stick. Cover tightly. Tear the red tissue into strips that are half as long as the *Rigid Wrap* and 2 inches wide. Remove the plastic food wrap from the inside of the bowl. Stir the diluted glue.

4. Place one strip of tissue across the bottom of the bowl and brush the diluted glue over the strip. Add another strip, overlapping the first slightly; brush with the diluted glue. Continue adding strips in this manner, using the tip of the brush to push the tissue into creases and folds. When the inside of the bowl is covered, brush a light coat of the diluted glue over the tissue strips. Allow to dry completely. Use a scissors to trim excess *Rigid Wrap* and tissue from the top edge of the bowl.

5. Cut a *Petifor* in half. Squeezing it in a "U" shape, rub the folded area over the gold *Rub-Ons*; the foam should be well coated with gold. Rub the *Petifor* over the tissue, highlighting the raised areas. Replenish the *Petifor* with gold as necessary.

6. Apply a coat of *Renaissance Foil Sealer* to the inside of the bowl. Allow to dry.

7. Apply red *Renaissance Foil Basecoat* to the outside of the bowl. Allow to dry.

8. Apply *Renaissance Foil Adhesive* over the red paint. Allow to dry to a tacky state. Apply a second coat of the adhesive, this time brushing in the opposite direction. Allow to dry to a tacky state.

9. Apply gold *Renaissance Foil*, shiny side up, to the adhesive. Use a cotton swab to push the foil into the uneven surface of the *Rigid Wrap*; place and lift the foil until the desired coverage is achieved. If a crackled finish is desired, apply *Renaissance Foil Crackle Medium* to the foil as directed on the package.

10. Apply *Renaissance Sealer* over the outside of the bowl. Allow to dry.

Faux Paste Paper

Follow the instructions for paste paper, diluting and coloring the paste and preparing the paper and work surface (see Chapter 2). A white glue usually does not have to be diluted, but dilute tacky glues with water to the consistency of sour cream. Either paste or an acrylic medium can be blended with white or tacky glues; again, dilute the blend to the consistency of sour cream. Twinrocker *Slow Drying Glue* is a premixed PVA/methyl cellulose blend that does not have to be diluted and is excellent for faux paste paper. If the glue you have diluted feels sticky when dry, apply an acrylic finish (brush or spray) to the paper.

Basic Collage and Assemblage

A collage is a design made by bonding various materials or objects to a larger surface. Generally the surface is either paper or wood, although any type of surface can be used. Decorated paper (purchased or self-made) frequently is bonded to the surface to provide background for the collage. It is not necessary that the items used in the collage completely cover the background.

An assemblage is similar to a collage; however, in an assemblage the finished results are more dimensional due to the types of materials and objects used. Assemblage designs frequently are done in a container with sides. Popular containers are all types of small wooden, tin and cardboard boxes, including flat candy tins and cigar boxes. Glass-covered shadow boxes are used to create an assemblage containing photos and memorabilia.

Select an adhesive suitable for the items included in a collage or an assemblage. Because these items do not receive heavy handling, adhesives forming a light bond usually are adequate. If you have had frustrating experiences when creating designs in either of these activities, Sue Pickering Rothamel's Book, *The Art Of Paper Collage* (refer to Inspirations) is an excellent source of techniques and tips. An example of a collage created by Sue can be seen on page 43.

Technique

Basic Decoupage

The term decoupage is derived from the French verb *decouper*, to cut out. A single motif or a grouping of motifs are cut from paper, glued to a surface (paper, fabric, wood, metal, glass, ceramic, etc.), and coated either with the glue or a sealant. In some cases, several coats of the glue or sealant are applied to the finished item; each coat is lightly sanded after it is dry.

1. When cutting out the motifs, hold the scissors stable with the points held directly in front of you. To get used to holding scissors in this position, hold the arm of your cutting hand on your hip. Rotate the motif, not the scissors, as you cut. Angle your cutting hand so the palm is slightly up-turned under the motif as you're cutting. This will grade the edge as you cut and will eliminate white showing around the cut edges of the motif.

2. The selected surface must be clean, dry, and free of oil and grease. Lightly sand wood, then wipe it off with a tack cloth.

3. Using the cut-out motifs, arrange a "test" design on the surface. Remove the motifs when pleased with the results.

4. Dilute the glue with water (distilled is recommended) to a consistency that is easily spread or brushed over the paper, usually about the thickness of sour cream.

5. Place the motifs, back up, on a non-stick work surface. Using your fingers or a small brush, apply a small amount of the diluted glue to the back of a motif.

6. Pick up the motif and position it on the surface. Using a long-handled-tweezers is handy if the pieces are small. Beginning at the center of the motif, and going to the outer edges, gently apply pressure either with the small brush or your fingertip. Remove any glue that seeps from under the edges with the tip of a cosmetic sponge or a cotton swab.

7. Using a small, dry brush, tap the motif securely to the surface. If bubbles form, pop them with the point of a pin and smooth the motif flat.

8. Continue adding motifs in this manner until all are in place. Allow to dry.

9. If desired, one or more coats of glue can be applied over the motifs. Allow a coat to dry, then lightly sand either with Houston Art & Frame *Super Film*, sandpaper labeled Very Fine Grade, or #0000 steel wool; wipe off the surface with a slightly damp cloth following each sanding.

10. Application of an acrylic finish is optional.

Note: Products that are both a glue and a sealant are described in Chapter 11.

Technique

Molded Excelsior Embellishments

Excelsior (natural or colored), glue, and open-backed cookie cutters quickly create use-anywhere embellishments. Any size cookie cutter can be used; the thickness is determined by the amount of excelsior placed into the cookie cutter. Remember, after being used for crafting, the cookie cutter should not be used again for cookie making.

1. Firmly press excelsior into an open-backed cookie cutter until the amount is slightly more than desired thickness. For use on paper projects, a depth of 1/8 to 1/4 inch is usually sufficient. For use as a holiday ornament, the cookie cutter can be filled to the top rim. Remove the excelsior.

2. Dilute glue (white or tacky) with water so that it is the consistency of cream (slightly thicker than water). You will need approximately 1/2 cup of the glue/water blend for each cup of excelsior.

3. Place the excelsior into a zip closure plastic bag. Pour the glue/water blend into the bag, over the excelsior; close the bag. Knead the bag so that all of the excelsior is dampened with the blend. Set aside for three hours (it can be placed in the refrigerator for up to one week).

4. To make the embellishment: Lightly spray the inside edges of the cookie cutter with cooking spray or rub a small amount of vegetable oil over the inside edges; place on a non-stick work surface. Knead the contents of the bag again. Open the bag and squeeze the excess glue/water blend from the excelsior. Place the excelsior into the cookie cutter, packing it down as much as possible. Set aside until both the top and bottom surfaces feel dry to the touch (placing it on a rack or plastic berry box will hasten drying). Gently push the excelsior from the cookie cutter; set aside until completely dry. Clip off any loose pieces of excelsior from the edges. Painting the embellishment is optional.

5. To use as an embellishment on paper, apply either white or tacky glue to the back of the embellishment.

6. To use as a hanging ornament; thread a darning needle with a doubled piece of colored wire and push it through the excelsior from the bottom to the top; twist the two ends of the wire together, at the bottom of the ornament. Pull the loop so the twisted ends are against to the bottom of the ornament.

Project

Heart Gift Basket

The heart-shaped "cookies" decorating the rim of this gift basket look good enough to eat! Clean-up is easy, because the mixing bowl is a plastic bag.

You Will Need

Painted fruit basket
6 Tablespoons (generous) Aleene's *Original Tacky Glue*
6 Tablespoons (scant) ground cinnamon
Medium or large primitive heart shapes Off The Beaten Track Cookie Cutters
Two pieces of cooking parchment paper
Roller (piece of PVC pipe, glass, etc.)
Plastic food bags (zip closure is best)
Optional: cinnamon oil, small brush, cookie sheet, oven

---

1. Place the cinnamon in the plastic bag; add the glue (dipping the tablespoon in water before measuring it will aid in removing it from the spoon). **Optional:** Three drops of cinnamon oil can be added if a stronger cinnamon odor is desired. Leaving the bag slightly open, knead until the glue is brown. Close the bag and set aside for three hours. **Note:** The mix can be left in the closed bag up to two days.

2. Open the bag slightly and knead until the glue has absorbed the cinnamon.

3. Place a piece of cooking parchment paper on a flat surface. Cut the side of the bag open, remove the glue/cinnamon mix, and place it on the parchment paper. If the mix is sticky, sprinkle a small amount of cinnamon over it; if dry and brittle, add a few drops of water. Flatten the mix with the palm of your hand.

4. Roll out the mix to a 1/8-inch thickness. Using the cookie cutters, cut the heart shapes; if necessary, use the tip of your finger to gently push the mix from the cutter. Place the cut-out "cookies" on the second piece of cooking parchment paper. Form scrap pieces of mix into a ball; roll flat and cut with the cookie cutter. Smooth the tops of the cookies by dampening your fingertip with water and rubbing it gently across the tops.

5. The cookies can either air-dry or be placed in a 100-degree on a cookie sheet in the oven for one hour.

6. **Optional:** If "frosting" is desired, dilute glue to a water-thin consistency, brush it over the top of each dried cookie, and sprinkle with cinnamon. Allow to dry and shake off any excess cinnamon.

7. Place a large drop of glue in the center back of each cookie. Position the cookies along the rim of the basket. Allow to dry.

Chapter 4

Clear Glues

Clear glues are water-based, non-toxic, synthetic adhesives intended for porous surfaces. They are water-reversible. When dry, some remove as easily from a surface as mucilage (see page 18), yet they differ from it in three ways: they are less susceptible to humidity, more flexible when dry, and do not discolor or turn brittle over time.

A wide range of products qualify as clear glues, including liquids in bottles and tubes (basting, photo, and envelope glues and collage gel), glue sticks, and glitter glues. The clear glues described in this chapter are not suitable for projects that will be laundered or dry cleaned, placed in an area with high moisture, or placed outdoors.

Clear glues in bottles and tubes have viscosities ranging from medium to thick. The bottles usually have some sort of applicator top. For example, Aleene's *Memory Glue* has a fine-line applicator tip on the bottle, and a brush top is included in the package. Tubes have either a sponge tip or a small opening at one end through which the glue is squeezed.

Clear glues form a medium bond. Those with a thicker viscosity—gel, basting, and photo glues—have a stronger tack and are slightly more flexible when dry. These glues set quickly; drying time for the thinner viscosities is a little less than that of the thicker viscosities. When applied in a very thin coat, most clear glues will neither wrinkle nor show through paper; however, it is best to test if using tissue paper or vellum.

Application

To apply clear glue, spread a thin coat over either the entire back, or one or all edges, of the paper being bonded to another surface. Using one of the tools suggested for use with paste (see Chapter 2), remove excess glue; the remaining glue should be evenly spread and barely visible. Position the glued paper on the surface to which it is being bonded; burnish as recommended for paste. Heavier papers should be weighted down until the glue is dry.

Paper, fabric, or wood can be glued to small wooden shapes with clear glues. Apply a slightly thicker coat to the wood than for paper. Lightly burnish the top of the wooden shape, and immediately wipe away any excess that oozes from the sides with a cotton swab. Burnish a second time to secure the shape to the surface to which it is being bonded. Weighting the surface down until the glue is dry is recommended.

Select either a basting, photo glue, or collage gel when bonding fabric to fabric, paper, or wood. Apply a light coat of glue to the back of the fabric; all edges must be coated with the glue. Avoid pushing the glue into the fibers of fabric; you should not see any glue on the fabric's right side. Position the fabric on the surface to which it is being bonded. Beginning at the center of the fabric piece and working out to the edges, burnish to secure the fabric to the surface. Immediately wipe away any glue that oozes from the edges. Burnish lightly again to secure the fabric to the surface to which it is being bonded.

Many of the clear glues packaged in bottles are suitable to use for collage, decoupage, and assemblage; some can be used for making paste paper. Other than assemblage, an acrylic finish is recommended when used for these techniques.

Crafter's Pick *Basting Glue* is removed from fabric by laundering; however, it is not affected by dry cleaning and can be used as a permanent glue for dry-clean-only fabrics.

Tightly cap containers of liquid clear glues when finished working. Store out of direct sunlight, away from heat and cold. The shelf life of these glues is approximately one year.

Brands of clear glue in bottles or tubes include:
- Aleene's *Memory Glue*
- Beacon *Mounting Adhesive*
- Crafter's Pick *Basting Glue, Collage Gel*, and *Memory Mount*
- Ross *Clear School Gel*
- Tombow *MonoAqua*
- UHU *Liquid Glue Pen* and *Office Pen*

Glue Sticks

Glue sticks are either clear, slightly tinted, or colored. The clear and tinted sticks dry clear, while those of a deeper color remain that color when dry. The product's label will indicate if it will dry clear.

Glue sticks are available in repositionable and permanent types. Both types dry very quickly and are easily removed from surfaces with a damp cloth. They have a light tack, and depending on the brand, the bond is light to medium.

Although suitable for all porous surfaces, they are primarily used for paper bonding. Those intended for use on photographs are formulated for glossy, semi-porous paper (vellum) and glossy, non-porous photo paper. Tombow *Glue Sticks* (both colored and clear) bond most vellum papers without being visible through the top sheet. Test before beginning and apply only the amount needed for bonding, because excessive glue will be visible.

Replace the cap tightly on a glue stick tube. Store in a closed plastic bag, out of sunlight, and away from heat and cold. Glue sticks have a shelf life of six to twelve months.

Repositionable glue sticks are covered in Chapter 6.

Brands of glue sticks in round, twist-up tubes include:
- Dritz *Craft/Sewing Glue Stick*
- Ross *Gel Stik* and *Stik*
- Tombow *Color Glue Stick* (dries clear) and *Glue Stick*
- UHU *Stic* (clear and tinted)

Brands of glue sticks in oval, push-up tubes include:
- UHU *Stic Photo, Envelope Sealer, Glue Stick*, and *Pop Up Stic* (available in colors)

Glitter Glues

These glues are intended for porous surfaces and often have a clear glue base, while glitter paints have an acrylic base and perform differently. Uses for glitter paints are included in Chapter 5. Glitter glues can be used for decorative and embellishment purposes but will not bond one surface to another.

Shake the glue container well before using. To help the flow in applicator bottles or tubes, shake with the tip down. If the tip becomes clogged, run a small piece of wire or an opened paper clip down the opening. If the glue has dried in the tip, remove the tip and rinse it clean in warm water.

Test before using glitter glue with thin paper; some may cause wrinkling. To use with fabric, push the glue into the fibers by dragging the tip of the applicator on the fabric. Glitter glue can be applied to finished wood, although it should be sanded lightly prior to applying the glue.

When only a hint of glitter is desired, apply with a small brush (not foam or sponge). The glue also can be applied with an applicator tip into the open areas of a stencil. Results are usually better if the glue is applied in several light coats, rather than one thick one.

Although glitter glue cannot be used to bond one surface to another, the following embellishing supplies will bond to it: Magicalfaerieland *Faerie Glass* (tiny glass beads without holes) and powdered mica pigments (Magicalfaerieland *Faerie Dust*, Jacquard Products *Pearl Ex,* Lemon Tree *Powdered Pearls*, and Twinrocker *Pearlescent Dry Pigments*). Apply the glue (by applicator tip, bristle brush, or rubber brayer) in a heavy coat so the supply will be securely bonded to the glue. Immediately sprinkle the supply on the glue; glitter glue dries very quickly.

Remove glitter glue spills while the glue is still wet; when dry, it is not as easily removed as liquid clear glues or glue sticks. After use, wipe off the tip and securely replace the top on the container. Store containers tip down. Glitter glue has a shelf life of approximately one year.

> **Brands of glitter glue include:**
> - **Clearsnap** *StarWriters*
> - **Crayola** *Glitter Glue*
> - **Duncan** *Glitter Writers*
> - **Ranger Industries, Inc.** *Stickles*
> - **Ross** *Glitter Glu*
> - **Suze Weinberg** *Putting On The Glitz*
> - **UHU** *Glitter Glue*

Technique

Self-made Glitter Stickers

The combination of paper punches, glitter glue, and envelope glue result in easy-to-make stickers. Glitter or powdered mica pigments can be sprinkled over the wet glitter glue to provide more glitz and sparkle.

> ### You Will Need
> One half sheet of sketch paper (colored card stock can be substituted)
> Twinrocker's *Remoistenable Glue*
> Duncan *Glitter Writers* in the colors of your choice
> Scratch-Art Rubber Brayer (hard or soft)
> McGill, Inc. Paper Punches in the sizes and shapes of your choice
> Two pieces of freezer paper or cooking parchment to use as a non-stick surface
> Optional: Createx Colors Glitter

1. Shake the bottle of *Glitter Writers* well. Squirt a 2-inch puddle of glitter glue on one non-stick surface. Roll the brayer through the glue until it is evenly coated.
2. Roll the glitter glue over the front of the paper to evenly coat it with the glitter glue. If more glitter is desired, sprinkle glitter over the wet glue. Allow to dry.
3. Squirt a 2-inch puddle of *Remoistenable Glue* on the second non-stick surface. Roll the brayer through the glue. If the brayer is not evenly coated with the glue, roll it over a clean area of the surface two or three times. Roll the glue over the back of the paper; the application should be even over the surface of the paper. Allow to dry.
4. Place the paper in the punch with the glitter side down, and punch out the designs. To use as a stickers, moisten the glue on the back of the punched design.

Chapter 5

Acrylic-based Adhesives

Acrylic-based adhesives differ from other water-based, non-toxic adhesives because they are not water-reversible. While still wet, they can be removed easily from surfaces, yet when dry, they are very difficult to remove. In addition to acrylic-based adhesives, this chapter includes information about acrylic mediums and acrylic-based paints and how those products also can be used as adhesives.

Each of these acrylic products—adhesives, mediums, and paints—contains acrylic polymers and shares acrylic polymer properties. They remain flexible and do not become brittle over time, and they rarely are affected by heat or moisture. Additionally, many are UV-resistant. Those without a pigment are white when wet and dry clear; those with a pigment (paints) dry to a color very close to the wet color.

When using products packaged in jars or wide-top bottles, remove the needed amount from the container with either a clean spoon or craft stick and place on a non-stick work surface. Those in applicator-tip bottles are generally applied directly from the bottle. Replace tops and lids as quickly as possible to prevent the product from drying out.

Although they are water-resistant, the adhesives are not waterproof. Unless noted to the contrary on the label, do not use these products on items that will be either submerged in water for long periods of time or displayed outdoors.

Prior to drying, remove acrylic products from surfaces with soap and water. If unable to clean up spills or tools immediately, keep acrylic-based products damp so they cannot dry: place rubber stamps on a damp kitchen sponge, wrap brushes and other applicator tools in wet paper towels and then in plastic food wrap, cover work surfaces with wet paper towels, and dampen clothing and carpeting. Attend to clean-up as quickly as possible.

If an acrylic should dry, General Pencil's *The Master's Brush Cleaner* will remove acrylics from bristle brushes, while *KissOff Stain Remover* safely removes dried acrylics from rubber stamps, rubber brayers, and most fibers (clothing, carpet, etc.). Rubbing alcohol or a solvent-based cleaner can also be used to clean tools and surfaces not affected by these supplies; dry cleaning removes acrylics from clothing.

Acrylic-based adhesives have an extended open time, allowing for the repositioning of the surfaces being bonded. Tack increases as the adhesive becomes set; drying time is usually short after set begins. They dry to a durable finish, and flex varies by brand.

These adhesives are suitable for several surfaces. Read the label carefully, because not all are suitable for fabric that will be laundered or dry-cleaned. Slick, shiny, or polished non-porous surfaces may need some roughing up with fine sand paper; that information will be on the label. Test when bonding a porous surface to a non-porous surface; generally, the adhesive must be applied to the porous surface.

Some porous surfaces may require sealing prior to applying the adhesive; sealing prevents the adhesive from soaking or seeping through thin surfaces. To use an acrylic adhesive as a sealer, apply a very thin coat to one or both surfaces. Allow to dry completely, then apply a second coat of the adhesive to one surface, and bond the surfaces together.

Each brand has specific instructions for the successful use of the product. Read and follow them. In general, the following applies to all acrylic-based adhesives:

• The best method of application is often that followed when applying paste to a surface (see Chapter 2). Remove excess adhesive in the same manner and use the same tools as directed for removing excess paste. When Daige *Rollataq 300 Adhesive System* is applied from the *Rollataq* dispenser, removing excess adhesive is not necessary; it applies the amount needed for bonding.

• Burnishing bonded areas after they have been positioned is recommended.

• Weighting down heavier surfaces until the adhesive has dried may be necessary.

• Test when using thin (tissue) and translucent (vellum) papers. Some adhesives may soak through or show through these papers.

• Several acrylic adhesives are designed to be used as both an adhesive and finish. The label will contain that information.

• The coloring supplies mentioned for natural adhesives (see Chapter 2) also can be used to color acrylic-based adhesives.

Brands of acrylic-based adhesives include:
• **Art Institute** *Dries Clear*
• **Beedz** *Shimmerz*
• **Daige** *Rollataq System*
• **Jones Tones** *Plexi 400*
• **Roo Products, Inc.** *RooClear, RooTac*, **and** *RooWood Glue*
• **USArt Quest** *Perfect Paper Adhesive* **(available in matte and gloss)**

Project

"And, It Was Written..."

Designed by Susan Pickering Rothamel, USArt Quest

Sue's designs are noted for their beauty and originality. Highly regarded, she is an artist in every respect. The finished size of this piece is 11-1/2 x 12 inches; however, it can be made in any size.

You Will Need

ClayWorks: Black*
Rubber stamp (©Stamp Out Cute)
Perfect Paper Adhesive (PPA) in matte*
Duo Embellishing Adhesive
Ah, That's Great Tape
Pearl Ex: Antique Copper*
Prefect fx: Antique Bronze*
Variegated Gildenglitz
Selected papers for the outer framework
Chiri art paper

Ogura lace paper
Pukka and Papel Skeleton Leaves*
WireWorks Gold and Olive Twigs*
Small sticks*
Small silk leaves*
Canula Berry Enhancements*
Miscellaneous supplies: *Rolling Pin*,
    small brush, craft knife, emery board,
    Texture Sponge
*Available from USArt Quest

1. Using the *Rolling Pin*, roll *ClayWorks* flat. Press the stamp into the clay; remove the stamp. Allow the clay to air dry. Lightly carve the stamped clay with the craft knife and emery board.
2. Mix the *PPA* with *Pearl Ex*. Paint the surface of the stamped clay. Allow to dry.
3. Brush *Duo Embellishing Adhesive* in strategic areas of the stamped clay; allow to dry until tacky. Place *Gildenglitz* on the adhesive; gently rub the leaf to secure it to the adhesive.
4. Thin the *PPA/Pearl Ex* mixture. Using the *Texture Brush*, glaze the entire surface of the clay. Allow to dry.
5. Bond the outer framework papers together with *Ah, That's Great Tape*; apply the framework to a stable substrate (i.e. a mat board) with the tape. Using *PPA*, create a collage with the lace paper, skeleton leaves, and art papers. Apply a thin coat of *PPA* over the surface of the collage; apply *Perfect fx* to the wet *PPA*. Allow to dry.
6. Glaze the sticks with the *PPA/Pearl Ex* mixture; add *WireWorks* twigs. Allow to dry.
7. Coat the silk leaves with *Duo Embellishing Adhesive*; apply *Gildenglitz* and Canula Berry Enhancements after the adhesive becomes tacky.
8. Using *PPA*, bond the clay tablet and the branch to the collage.

Project

Foiled Clay Flower Pot

Designed by Jones Tones

A clay pot filled with dried flowers becomes an admired decoration when the rim of the pot is decorated with a foiled design. Smaller sized pots with foiled rims are excellent table favors for showers.

You Will Need
Clay flower pot
Jones Tones *Plexi 400*
Jones Tones *Press On Iron-On Foil*:
   Copper
Dried flowers
Rubbing alcohol
Optional: florist clay, wooden skewer

1. Wipe off the rim of the pot with rubbing alcohol to remove any dirt or oils. Place the pot in a 125-degree oven for 30 minutes. Allow to cool.
2. Using the tip of the *Plexi 400* bottle, apply a repetitious, linear design along the rim. Allow to dry until clear.
3. Place the foil on the adhesive, shiny side up. Gently rub the foil on the raised lines of the design; lift the clear sheet covering the foil. Repeat as necessary to cover all areas of the adhesive with foil.
4. Fill the pot with flowers. If florist clay is placed in the pot for weight, poke holes in the clay with the skewer for the stems of the flowers.

Beaded Christmas Tree Ornament

No stitching is required for this beaded beauty! This easily made ornament is perfect when time is short and the gift list is long.

> ### You Will Need
> Art Accents *Treasure Beadz* in the color of your choice
> Art Accents *Beadz Shimmerz*
> Bostik *Blu Tack*
> Darice *Embossing Essentials Double-Sided Adhesive Film*
> Two ColArt Americas *Glass & Tile Colors* Glass Large Diamonds
> Short piece of decorative cording
> Miscellaneous supplies: rubbing alcohol, plastic plate with sides

1. Place one diamond shape on the release paper covering the double-sided adhesive film. Trace the shape on the release paper. Without removing the paper, cut along the traced lines. Set aside.
2. Wipe off both sides of the diamond shapes with rubbing alcohol. Allow to dry. Place a small piece of *Blu Tack* removable adhesive in the center back of each diamond.
3. Pour a heavy layer of *Treasure Beadz* onto the plastic plate. Apply a heavy coating of *Shimmerz* to the front of one diamond. Using the removable adhesive as a handle, place the diamond, glue side down, on the *Treasure Beadz*. Press the diamond firmly into the *Treasure Beadz*. Pick up the diamond shape and place it beaded side up on a flat surface. Repeat for the second diamond, adding more

Treasure Beadz to the plate if necessary. Allow both diamonds to dry.
4. Remove the *BluTack* from the back of each diamond shape. Wipe off the back of the shape with rubbing alcohol, taking care not to get alcohol on the *Shimmerz*. Remove the release paper from one side of the traced adhesive film. Place the film on the back of one diamond. Remove the remaining release paper from the film; place a folded piece of decorative cording on the film to form a loop at the top of the diamond. Position the second diamond on the film; press the two diamonds together firmly with your fingers.
5. Spread *Shimmerz* along the outer edges of the joined diamonds. Dip the sides of the diamonds into the *Treasure Beadz* on the plate (adding more, if necessary). Allow to dry.

Acrylic Mediums

Acrylic mediums bond porous surfaces to porous surfaces. Some bond porous surfaces to semi-porous and non-porous surfaces, but the medium must be applied to the porous surface. Test to determine if the results will be satisfactory.

Apply acrylic mediums in the same manner followed for acrylic-based adhesives. Most have slightly more open time (see Chapter 1) than the adhesives. Textile mediums dry the most flexible and can be used on all porous surfaces; gloss medium has slightly less flex when dry.

The options offered by acrylic mediums are endless. In addition to their uses as an adhesive, finish, and glaze, they also are binders for dry powdered mica and liquid pigments (see Chapter 2).

Mediums can be used either as a clear finish or a tinted glaze; however, an acrylic varnish provides a slightly more durable finish than a medium. Available in gloss and matte, varnishes can be applied as either a clear finish or tinted glaze over acrylic adhesives and mediums, natural adhesives, PVA (white) glues and tacky glues that feel sticky when dry. Apply a UV-resistant varnish over projects when that feature is desired.

Apply clear finish and tinted glaze in a thin coat. If dilution is necessary, follow the manufacturer's instructions; some require dilution with an extender rather than water. If applying multiple coats, allow each coat to dry thoroughly before applying the next.

The tinted glaze and paint that results when an acrylic medium and coloring supply are mixed together is permanent and has the adhesive properties of the medium. Coloring supplies suitable for use with acrylic mediums are those mentioned for natural adhesives (see Chapter 2).

Gel mediums have a thick viscosity and are available either plain or with added substances, like glass beads, black flint, and sand. Impasto mediums are a thicker viscosity and are used to create dimension and texture.

Modeling paste is very thick and generally is applied with some type of stable-edged tool. Modeling paste can be applied over either plastic or metal stencils on a porous surface.

Createx Colors offers a variety of acrylic products, including *Gloss Medium*, *Textile Medium*, *Lyntex Paper Medium*, *Matte Medium*, and *Soft Gel Medium*. To make paint to use on fabric, mix Createx Colors *Fabric Medium* with Createx Colors *Pure Pigment*; heat-set either with an iron or heat gun after the paint has dried. All Createx Colors mediums can be colored with *Pure Pigment* or one of the other suggested coloring supplies.

Acrylic mediums and acrylic paints do not stick to craft foam, making it the perfect supply for self-made dimensional stencils. Make stencils by punching or cutting designs in the foam (another option is a trip to the closest store having an Accu-Cut machine). Spray a repositionable adhesive to one side of the foam stencil and allow to dry; apply spray a second time and allow to dry. Place the stencil, adhesive side down, on the surface. Burnish the stencil securely to the surface with either a Clover Needlecraft, Inc. *Finger Presser*, Scratch Art *Rubbing Stick*, or the back of a plastic spoon.

Apply either a heavy-bodied acrylic medium or dimensional fabric paint over the stencil with an etchall *squeegee* or charge card. Using the same tool, pull the medium or paint over the stencil; the acrylic should fill all open areas of the stencil and be level with the back of the stencil. Pick up the stencil immediately. If desired, acrylic mediums can be colored prior to applying. Glitter can be sprinkled over the medium or paint before lifting the stencil.

Winsor & Newton's wide range of acrylic products include *Matte Medium*, *Gloss Medium*, *Gloss Gel*, *Matt Gel*, *Impasto Medium*, *Iridescent Medium*, *Fine Texture Gel*, *Coarse Textured Gel*, *Pumice Textured Gel*, *Natural Sand Gel*, *Black Flint Gel*, *Glass Beads Gel*, *Modeling Paste*, *Gloss Varnish*, and *Matt Varnish*. When coloring is desired, use any of the suggested coloring supplies (see page 16).

Technique

Faux Metal Heart Pin

A pre-cut mat board heart, a little tissue paper, some acrylic medium and stamping inks combine to create a pin. It can be left unadorned, although decorating it is great fun. If a pin isn't in your plan, the heart can be used as a gift tag.

You Will Need

3-inch pre-cut primitive heart in non glossy mat board

One quarter sheet Bemiss-Jason *Antique Gold Luster Tissue*

Winsor & Newton *Modeling Paste*

Scratch Art *Leaves Texture Plate*

Clearsnap, Inc. *MetalExtra Pigment Ink Pads*: Verdigris and Burnt Copper

4-inch square Sulky *Iron-On Interfacing*: Black

Self-adhesive pin back or 6-inch piece of decorative cording for gift tag

Assorted embellishments (colored wire, jewels, ribbons, paper beads, charms, buttons, feathers, etc)

Non-stick work surface

Miscellaneous supplies: Ball point pen or fine line marker, small scissors, sheet of white tissue paper, iron, ironing board, 1/16-inch hole punch, craft stick, white pen for gift tag

Optional: heat gun

1. Use the craft stick to scoop out approximately one teaspoon of *Modeling Paste* from the jar and place it on the work surface; set aside. Mark an X on one side of the heart. Place the X marked side up on the *Luster Tissue*. Make two tracings of the heart on the tissue. Cut out one heart shape along the traced lines. Cut out the second heart shape, leaving slightly more than 1/8 inch beyond the traced lines. With the X marked side down, trace the heart on the wrong side of the interfacing (the milky colored side). Cut out along the traced lines. Set the interfacing heart aside.

2. Using the craft stick, spread a coating of *Modeling Paste* over the X marked side of the mat board heart. The coating should be slightly more than 1/8 inch thick. Place the first heart cut from the *Luster Tissue* (the smaller of the two) over the *Modeling Paste*. Apply a thin coating of *Modeling Paste* over the tissue paper; the coating should not be more than 1/8 inch thick. Cover with the second heart cut from the *Luster Tissue* (the larger of the two). Wrap the edges of the tissue paper over the edges of the mat board, to the back. Using the craft stick, smooth the tissue paper to the edges of the mat board heart. It may be necessary to make a small clip in the valley at the top of the heart so that the tissue paper conforms to the shape. Use the side of the craft stick to smooth the edges of the heart and to flatten the tissue paper on the back of the heart.

3. Holding the *Verdigris Pigment Ink Pad* ink side down (parallel to the heart), lightly pat the pad on the tissue paper so that the paper is covered with a layer of ink. Set the heart aside for 30 minutes.

4. Pat the *Verdigris Pigment Ink Pad* over the surface of the *Leaves Texture Plate*. Place the heart, tissue side up, on the work surface and cover with the *Texture Plate*. Gently press the plate into the tissue. Remove the plate.

5. Heat the iron to a medium setting. Place a double thickness of white tissue paper on the ironing board. Place the heart, tissue side down, on the paper and cover with a double thickness of white tissue paper. Using light pressure, press the back of the heart until the *Modeling Paste* is almost firm. Remove the heart from the ironing board. **Note:** If using a heat gun, place the heart right side up on the ironing board and heat until the *Modeling Paste* is almost firm.

6. Lightly pat the *Burnt Copper Pigment Ink Pad* over the front of the heart. Use light pressure to avoid getting the ink into the recessed areas of the *Modeling Paste*. Place the heart on the ironing board, right side up, and cover with white tissue paper. Lightly press the heart to set the ink. **Note:** If using a heat gun, do not cover the heart with white tissue paper.

7. Turn the heart over on the white tissue paper. Place the heart traced from the interfacing on the back of the heart; the milky side is down. Press (a heat gun cannot be used for this) the interfacing to secure it to the back of the heart. Allow to cool. Do not add decorations until the *Modeling Paste* is firm and set (approximately 30 minutes).

Decorating the pin: Use the hole punch to make holes along either a portion or all outer edges of the heart. Lace colored wire, ribbon, or cording through the holes. String beads on any of these supplies to create dingle-dangles to hang from the edges. Small charms, buttons, or feathers can be attach with glue or an acrylic medium. When decorating is complete, add a pin back.

Making a gift tag: The tag can be decorated in the same manner as a pin or left "as is." Punch a hole in the valley at the top of the heart and string a piece of cording through the hole. Tie both ends. Use a white pen to write the recipient's and your name on the back of the heart and don't forget to add the date.

Technique

Really, Really Faux Paste Paper

No paste and no paper—but the results look as though both are used, and it can be used in the same way (see page 21). Consider these instructions just the beginning. Select the acrylic medium, coloring supplies, and type of stabilizer best suited to the ways you intend to use the "paper."

You Will Need	
Sulky *Cut-Away Plus Permanent Stabilizer*	Freezer paper
Createx Colors *Pure Pigment*: Blue	Miscellaneous supplies: foam brush, craft sticks, plastic picnic fork, disposable surface (plastic cover from coffee or yogurt)
Winsor & Newton *Medium Texture Gel*	
#8 Royal Brush MFG Co. *Stipple Brush*	
Twinrocker *Pearlescent Pigment*: Gold	Optional: double-sided adhesive film

1. Cut the stabilizer in the size needed for your project and place it on the shiny side of the freezer paper. Pour a small amount of the liquid pigment on the disposable surface. Using the foam brush, apply the pigment to the stabilizer.

2. Use a craft stick to scoop out approximately one tablespoon of the gel from the jar and place it on a small piece of freezer paper. Use the side of another craft stick to spread the gel over the surface of the stabilizer. The gel will become the color of the pigment as it is spread. The coating of gel should be somewhat even.

3. Place approximately 1/2 teaspoon of the pigment powder on a piece of freezer paper. Dip the end of the stipple brush into the dry pigment powder. Lightly shake the brush over the powder on the paper to remove some of excess. Holding the brush over the piece of stabilizer, tap the side of the brush to apply a light coating of powder over the gel. Repeat in this manner until the gel surface has a light coating of powder.

4. Using the plastic folk, run lines through the gel. The pigment powder will be barely visible. Add more powder to the gel as before. Use the back of the fork to smooth the surface of the gel and to blend the powder into the gel. Allow to dry flat.

5. Optional: A sheet of a double-sided adhesive film can be placed on the back of the stabilizer for mounting on another surface. If the stabilizer is to be cut into pieces to use as embellishing for paper art, apply the double-sided adhesive film before cutting.

Acrylic Paints

Acrylic paints are available for a wide range of surfaces, from paper to glass, in viscosities ranging from water thin to very thick. With the possible exception of those that are water-thin, acrylic paints can be used as an adhesive on all porous surfaces, most semi-porous surfaces, and some non-porous surfaces. Polymer (adhesion) + pigment (color) = colored glue. It's best to test to determine if the paint and surfaces being used are compatible for bonding.

Follow these guidelines when using acrylic paint as an adhesive:

• Unless noted to the contrary on the label, do not dilute acrylic paint with water; thin the paint with the extender for the brand of paint you have selected.

• Apply the paint in a thin coat when bonding papers.

• When using glass paint to bond embellishments (beads, glitter, etc.) to paper, wood, or glass, apply the embellishment immediately— glass paint dries very quickly.

• Select a paint suitable for non-porous surfaces when using plastic; some of these surfaces may require a sealer coat before the paint is applied (which will be indicated on the label).

• Before applying paint to fabric, press freezer paper to the wrong side of the fabric; leave in place until after heat setting. Paint must be pushed into the fibers of fabric. Drag the tip of the applicator bottle firmly along the fabric; do not "drip" the paint onto it. Heat-set with an iron or heat gun after the paint has dried unless noted to the contrary on the label.

• When bonding embellishments (beads, trims, etc.) to clothing, apply the paint thick enough to firmly secure the embellishment to the fabric. Allow to dry flat. Do not launder for at least one week.

• When bonding jewels to fabric, place a small puddle of paint where the jewel will be positioned; drop the jewel in the center of the puddle and push it firmly into the paint. The paint should squish up around the edges of the jewel. Allow to dry flat. Do not launder for at least one week.

• Glitter paint is better used as a decorative supply rather than a bonding supply. If used on clothing, do not launder for at least ten days.

Project

Greeting Card

The textured border on this card is easily created with puff paint. Using a card normally used for a photo eliminates the need to cut an opening.

You Will Need

Paper Adventures *Photo-Frame-Folding Card* in Mat

Rubber stamp: Lion Fish ©Mostly Animals used in example

White tissue paper (piece larger than opening in card)

Gum arabic (dry or pre-mixed)

Clearsnap, Inc, *Top Boss Embossing Ink*

Think Ink *Clear Liquid Glass*

Tulip *Puffy 3-D Paint*: White

Double-sided adhesive film

1/4-inch wide double-sided adhesive tape

Air Erasable Fine Line Marker from Clotilde

Miscellaneous tools: small brush, scissors, heat gun

1. The tissue should be smooth and flat; if necessary, press with an iron. With the card opened and face down on a flat surface, place the tissue over the card's opening. Lightly draw lines on the tissue that are 1/2 inch beyond each edge of the opening (the tissue will be 1 inch longer and 1 inch wider than the opening in the card). Pick up the tissue and cut along the marked lines on the tissue. Set aside.

2. Brush a medium coat of the *Puffy 3-D Paint* over the front frame area of the opening. Allow to dry overnight. Using a heat gun, puff the paint. Set aside.

3. Ink the stamp and print the image in the center of the tissue paper. Cover the print with embossing powder, shake off excess powder, and heat until melted.

4. If necessary, dilute the gum arabic with distilled water to the consistency of milk. Blend each re-inker color in gum arabic until the desired color is reached.

5. Place the print on a clean sheet of paper with the embossed side down. Dip the end of the small brush into the color selected for the center of the fish. Touch the brush lightly to the tissue. The color will spread, but will stop at the melted embossing powder which acts as a resist. Clean the brush in water and apply the next color. Continue in this manner until all areas of the tissue are colored. Allow to dry.

6. Place the card on a flat surface with the back of the opening up. Place a strip of 1/4-inch double-sided tape along each of the four sides of the opening. Position the tissue on the tape with the embossed side up. Finger-press the tissue to the tape.

7. Leaving both the liner and release in place, place a piece of double-sided adhesive film over the section of the card that will be behind the opening. Trim the film to the size of the card. Remove the liner from the film and place over the back of the opening (where the tissue is). Remove the release paper from the film and bring the back of the card over the film. Lightly burnish to secure the two sections of the card together.

8. Add a greeting to the back of the card.

Speedy Decorated Gift Papers and Tags

This decorated paper takes but a minute to make. Best of all, it's a good way to use up that lingering bit of paint; the amount that's too little to use, but too much to throw away.

You Will Need

Leftover dimensional acrylic craft paint
Any paper, from shelf to metallic
Scrap pieces of card stock
Kitchen sponge

1. Place the paper on a flat surface. Pour the paint onto a disposable, non-stick surface. Dip the end of the sponge in the paint and apply randomly over the paper. Allow to dry. Use as gift wrap.
2. Brush paint over one side of a piece of card stock; immediately cover with a piece of decorated paper. Burnish with a clean sponge. Allow to dry. Cut into rectangles, squares, or circles to use as gift tags.

Tulip Paper

No one will mistake this paper for hand-made, but it resembles the real thing. It's quickly made and handy to use as a background paper or for embellishing.

You Will Need

Tulip *Puffy 3-D Paint*: White
White tissue paper
Powdered mica pigments
Scratch-Art *Lolli Foam Brush*
Miscellaneous supplies: small mixing container, freezer paper, cookie sheet, clothespins, heat gun

1. Cover the cookie sheet with freezer paper, shiny side up. Secure the paper to the cookie sheet with clothespins. Place two sheets of tissue paper on the freezer paper; the tissue paper should be an inch narrower and shorter than the freezer paper on each side.
2. Mix equal amounts of the paint with water. Blend in powdered mica pigments to obtain the desired color.
3. Dip the end of the brush into the paint and tap it around the outer edges of the tissue paper to secure it to the freezer paper, replenishing the brush as necessary. After the edges are secure, tap paint over the entire surface of the tissue paper. If the paper tears, tap the torn edges down with the brush. The paper should be well saturated with the paint.
4. Using the heat gun, dry the tissue. If any bubbles occur, tap them down with the wet brush and reheat. When cool, remove the tissue paper from the freezer paper.

Note: More layers of tissue paper can be used if a thicker paper is desired; apply enough paint to saturate all layers of the tissue. For a puffier paper, allow the tissue to dry before heating with the gun.

Chapter 6
Repositionable and Removable Adhesives

There are two type of repositionable adhesives: those that are water-reversible and form a temporary bond, and those that are not water-reversible and are dual-use. Water-reversible adhesives are semi-solids in glue sticks or cake-form and liquid sprays. Those that are not water-reversible are liquids in applicator bottles, markers, pens, and sprays. Depending on the application method, dual-use adhesives form either a temporary or permanent bond.

In addition to being used to bond surfaces together, most dual-use adhesives also can be used as the adhesive, or size, for a variety of embellishments including metal leaf, craft foil, powdered mica pigments, and embossing powder (refer to Chapter 11, for instructions).

Removable adhesives are reusable. The putty-like substance can be used again and again until it is no longer sticky. It's frequently used to bond light- to medium-weight items to vertical surfaces (like doors and walls).

Repositionable films and tapes are described in Chapter 7; additional spray adhesives are described in Chapter 10.

Glue Sticks and Cake Forms

These forms of repositionable glue form a light bond and are generally used to bond paper to paper; however, Scotch *Restickable Glue Stick* is often used by rubber stampers to temporarily mount rubber dies on blocks. Generally, these adhesives remove easily from surfaces (including clothing) with warm water and soap.

Liquid Repositionable Adhesives

Liquid repositionable adhesives are packaged in bottles, as markers, and a rolling ball

---

Brands of glue sticks and cake forms include:
- **CPE** *Quick Stick Wax* (in cake form)
- **Ross** *Stick 'N Post*
- **Scotch** *Post-it Glue Stick* and *Restickable Glue Stick*

---

pen that offers the option of dual-use; if surfaces are joined immediately after the adhesive is applied, the bond is permanent, but if the adhesive is allowed to dry before the surfaces are joined, the bond is repositionable (temporary). A repositionable adhesive is dry when the color has become clear and the surface feels tacky.

The viscosity of those in applicator-tip bottles and jars ranges from thin to thick. The adhesive can be applied in a variety of ways, including an applicator-tip bottle, dauber-top bottle, brush, sponge, rubber stamp, rubber brayer, and the applicators seen on pages 11-13.

The marker or pen is the applicator for those brands of repositionable adhesives. These products are especially handy when a small area of repositionable glue is desired. The pen is often used for embellished or thermal embossed signatures or line drawings.

Clean up spills and tools before the glue dries—most are difficult to remove when dry. If unable to immediately remove the adhesive from tools, wrap them (including brushes) in wet paper towels, then in plastic food wrap; place rubber stamps on a wet kitchen sponge.

If the adhesive has dried, it can be removed from non-porous surfaces with rubbing alcohol (but test first—alcohol may damage the surface). General Pencil *The Master's Brush Cleaner* removes it from brushes, and *Kiss-Off Stain Remover* safely removes it from rubber stamps, rubber brayers, and most fibers (clothing and carpet). Dry cleaning also removes it from clothing.

Brands of liquid repositionable adhesives include:
- Aleene's *3-D Foiling Glue* and *Tack-It Over & Over*
- Anita's *Leaf Foiling* (available in a kit with foil and metal applicator top for bottle)
- B & B Etching Products, Inc. *etchadhesive*
- Delta *Stencil Magic Liquid Adhesive* and *Renaissance Foil Adhesive*
- Fiskars *2-way Photo Glue Marker*
- Frances Meyers Memories *2-in-1 Marker* and *2-in-1 Glue Pen*
- Houston Art & Frame, Inc. *Gold Leaf Adhesive Size* (solvent-based)
- Jones Tones *Plexi 400*
- Leeho *2 In 1 Glue Marker* by Sailor
- Magic Leaf *Special Bonding Agent* from Accent Import-Export
- Paper Adventures *Archival Glue Marker*
- Sailor *2 In 1 Rolling Ball Pen*
- Sunday International *Foil Magic Adhesive*
- Tombow *MonoMulti*
- USArt *Quest DuoAdhesive*

Project

Gold Leafed Frame

Thanks to composition leaf, a leafed frame is an easy-to-do, inexpensive project. When working, handle the leaf as little as possible, because the oils in your skin can tarnish it. To retain the leaf's color, apply a sealer to the finished frame.

1. Remove the acetate insert from the frame's opening. Trace the acetate on the card stock; set the acetate aside. Cut the card stock along the traced lines. Slide the cut card stock into the opening.

2. Working on a non-stick surface, apply an even coat of the adhesive to the front and sides of the frame with the small brush; allow to dry to a tacky state. Clean the brush immediately. Allow to dry before using in Step 7.

3. Slide the frame, front up, onto the white tissue paper (touching the adhesive may affect bonding). Swipe the ends of the bristles of the larger brush across the back of your hand. Using the ends of the bristles, pick up a piece of the leaf and place it on the top of the frame. As much as possible, do not touch the leaf with your fingers. Continue applying the leaf in this manner until the front and sides of the frame are covered.

4. Using the ends of the bristles of the larger brush, lightly tap the leaf to secure it to the adhesive. Excess leaf will fall on the tissue paper.

5. If any areas of the frame have bare spots, use the brush to pick up leaf from the tissue paper and reapply leaf to those areas. If it's necessary to apply additional adhesive, allow it to dry to a tacky state before applying leaf to those areas.

6. When the front and sides of the frame are covered with leaf, lightly burnish the leaf with the larger brush. Set the frame aside. Place the leftover pieces of leaf into a small paper or plastic box for use on another project.

7. Working on a non-stick surface, apply Sealer to all leafed areas of the frame. Set aside to dry. Remove the card stock from the opening. Slide the photograph into the opening; slide the acetate over the photograph.

Spray Repositionable Adhesives

Spray repositionable adhesives are available in water-reversible and water-resistant products. Those that are water-reversible can be removed from surfaces by soaking in warm, soapy water. Although primarily intended as a temporary bond for fabric projects, these products are excellent to use on non-porous surfaces when an easy-to-remove temporary adhesive is desired (the back of a stencil, for example). Before spraying, read the use of spray adhesives (see page 56). Although not water-reversible, Sulky KK2000 disappears from a surface within two to five days when exposed to air. Mineral spirits will remove the adhesive if removal is desired prior to that time. Additionally, this spray adhesive is neither flammable nor toxic.

Project

Leafed Candles

Leafed candles are safe to burn and turn a clearance table bargain into a stunning decoration. Before applying a repositionable spray adhesive to a candle, first wipe off the candle with alcohol and allow to dry. *Sulky KK2000* was used as the adhesive for both candles shown. This spray adhesive is "air-erasable"; if exposed to air, it disappears from a surface within two to five days; however, if covered, it retains its adhesive properties.

> ## You Will Need
> Pillar candle, color of your choice
> Metal leaf, color of your choice
> Sulky *KK2000*
> Rubbing alcohol or packaged alcohol
>   swabs
> 1-inch wide soft brush
> Miscellaneous supplies: small cloth
>   (for rubbing alcohol), sheet of
>   paper, small plastic bag, waxed
>   paper, tissue paper

For either method: Wipe off the surface of the candle with rubbing alcohol. Allow to dry.

For complete coverage: Place the candle in a spray box and spray the sides of the

candle with *KK2000*. Place the candle upright on a piece of scrap paper and cover the candle with the leaf. Additional spray can be applied if necessary. Remove excess leaf with a small brush. Use a small piece of waxed paper to burnish the leaf to the candle. Place the excess leaf on the scrap paper and place it in a plastic bag or box for future use.

For partial coverage: Tear white tissue paper into small pieces. Apply the torn tissue paper randomly to the sides of the candle; burnish them in place with your fingertip. Place the candle in a spray box and spray the sides of the candle. Place the candle upright on a piece of scrap paper. Cover the candle (and the pieces of tissue paper) with the leaf. Do not apply additional adhesive. Remove excess leaf with a soft brush and lift the tissue paper pieces from the candle. Use a small piece of waxed paper to burnish the leaf to the candle. Place the excess leaf on the scrap paper into a plastic bag or box for future use.

Water-resistant products are usually dual-use; the label will include that information. If surfaces are joined together immediately after one surface is sprayed with the adhesive, the bond is permanent, although it may be necessary to burnish the top surface to ensure a secure bond. If the adhesive is allowed to dry before the surfaces are joined, the bond is repositionable. Several types of embellishments can be applied to the repositionable bond (see Chapter 11 for instructions).

Labels on spray products include specific instructions for the proper use of the product. Read and follow those instructions; all have warnings and precautions and require adequate ventilation during use.

Removing water-resistant spray adhesives from surfaces is difficult. To avoid clean-up, use a large box turned on its side for a "spray box." The box should be at least 2 inches deeper than the distance recommended by the manufacturer when using the product. Shake the can well and spray the inside back wall. Allow to dry. Place flat items being sprayed on the adhesive (they also can be attached with removable adhesive mentioned later in this chapter). Direct the spray horizontally, then vertically, over the item. If a permanent bond is desired, remove the item and place it on the surface to which it is being bonded; burnishing is often necessary for a smooth, secure bond. If a temporary bond is desired, allow the adhesive to dry for the amount of time given on the label.

After spraying, turn the can upside down and hold the nozzle down until only air comes out (do this into the box). This cleans the nozzle and should be done each time the can is used. Should the nozzle become clogged, remove it and soak it in rubbing alcohol. It may be necessary to use a small pin to clean out the opening in the nozzle. **Do not** put the pin into the opening at the top of the can. If the spray got on surfaces where it wasn't wanted, use rubbing alcohol, mineral spirits, Ross *De-Solv-it* (a non-toxic cleaner), or UnDu Products *UnDu* to remove it.

Brands of water-resistant adhesives include:
- 3M *Photo Mount, Spray Mount,* and 3M *Super 77*
- Blair *Spray Adhesive*
- Bostik *Pressure Sensitive*
- Delta *Stencil Magic Spray Adhesive*
- Plaid *Laura Ashley Stencil Spray Adhesive*
- Sullivan *Art & Craft Spray*
- Surebonder *355 Spray Adhesive*

Project

Christmas Decorations

At one time, it was difficult finding clear glass balls to decorate at any time except Christmas. Crafts stores now have them in stock all year, allowing us the opportunity to avoid the last minute rush and create stunning decorations whenever we are in the mood. Begin by lightly coating the inside of a clear ball with glitter; two methods for adding more sparkle and color follow.

For Both Variations

1. Remove the cap from the top of the ball. Set aside. Holding the spray nozzle directly in the opening at the top of the ball, spray two or three short bursts of the adhesive into the ball. Cover the open top with the paper towel and shake the ball to disperse the adhesive evenly over the interior of the ball. Pour a small amount of glitter into the ball. Place the folded paper towel over the opening and shake the ball. Empty excess glitter from the ball. Replace the cap on the ball.

Variation 1

You Will Need
Supplies listed above
Small gold star stickers
Glitter glue

1. Repeat Step 1 above as many times as needed so that the inside of the ball is heavily coated with glitter. Excess glitter should be emptied before spraying additional adhesive on the ball. When finished, empty excess glitter from the ball.

To Lightly Coat the Inside of the Ball With Glitter You Will Need*
Clear glass ball with removable cap
Spray adhesive
Glitter (color of your choice)
Small piece of folded paper towel
   (use caution when handling the
   opening on the ball; it often has sharp
   and ragged edges)

*These supplies are used in both variations

2. Leaving the stickers on the release paper, apply glitter glue to each star. When dry, remove the stickers from the release paper and place them on the ball. Replace the cap on the ball.

Variation 2

You Will Need
Supplies listed on page 57

Two or three colors of powdered mica pigments: In the example Jacquard Products *Pearl Ex* Interference Blue/Green, Magicalfaerieland Shimmering Green *Faerie Dust* and Twinrocker *Pearlescent White* were used

Krylon *Webbing Spray*: White

Small craft stick

Miscellaneous supplies: Disposable plastic gloves or plastic bags, piece of scrap paper, small piece of cloth to wrap around ball

1. After lightly coating the inside of the ball with glitter, wrap it in a small cloth and spray white *Webbing Spray* into the opening in four short bursts. Rotate the ball a quarter turn with each burst. You may notice that the ball becomes very cold from the *Webbing Spray*.

2. Using the end of the small craft stick as a scope, place approximately 1/4 teaspoon of the lightest color of the mica pigment into the ball. Cover the end of the ball with the folded paper towel and shake the ball. Empty the excess mica pigment from the ball onto the scrap paper. Apply the other colors of mica pigment in the same way, emptying the excess of one color before adding another. Additional *Webbing Spray* can be sprayed into the ball if the mica pigments are not sticking to the inside of the ball.

3. Protecting your hands either with gloves or plastic bags, hold the ball by the opening and spray the outside of the ball with the *Webbing Spray*. Allow to dry. Replace the cap on the ball.

Products Having a Repositionable Adhesive Surface

Products with a repositionable adhesive surface also are available. 3M *Post-Its Notes* and *Flags* are found in a variety of colors, designs, and sizes. Another 3M product is the *Post-it Framed Bulletin Board*. The surface of the board is coated with a repositionable adhesive eliminating the need of pins. Not only is it a bulletin board for walls and the front of the refrigerator (mount the board on a magnetic sheet), it's also an excellent surface to use for planning paper or fabric designs.

Delta *Renaissance Instant Gilded Monograms* and *Designs* are repositionable on one side and permanent on the other. The permanent side is placed on a surface, and Delta *Renaissance Foil* is applied to the repositionable side.

Avant'CARD *Magic Mesh* products are double sided (both the front and back of the mesh have a repositionable adhesive). *Magic Mesh* is available in a variety of mesh sizes, in several colors and can be thermal embossed.

Manco has several double-sided repositionable products: *Lok-Lift Rug Gripper* (in 2-1/2- and 10-inch widths), *Removable Clear Mounting Tabs* (one side is permanent), *Wall Repair Patch Wall Repair Tape*, and *Indoor/ Outdoor Carpet Tape*. Manco *Wall Repair Patch* and *Wall Repair Tape* can be thermal embossed. Position the selected product on the intended surface, then sprinkle embossing powder over it. Shake off the excess powder and heat until melted. Additional information concerning thermal embossing is found in Chapter 9.

Removable Adhesives

Removable adhesives are putty-like. The needed amount is cut easily with scissors or pulled from a larger piece. This type of adhesive can be used in place of a magnet and is especially handy for those places where a magnet can't be used. The packaging for each brand recommends the maximum weight that can be supported and the amount needed for that weight.

The adhesive is heat-sensitive and should not be used where it will be exposed to direct sunlight or by a heat source. Some will stain painted walls if left in place for extended periods; that information will be on the label.

A piece of removable adhesive placed on the end of a pen cap, pencil, or piece of dowel that has been placed in STYROFOAM is the perfect drying "platform" for small items. The item will be held in a stable position until dry.

Needless to say, the adhesive is excellent for cleaning up glitter, beads, embossing powder, dry pigment spills, and nearly any small item. Form the adhesive into a ball and roll to make a snake. Roll the snake over the surface being cleaned.

Brands of removable adhesive include:
- Bostik *Blu-Tac Adhesive*
- CPE *Stay Putty*
- Ross *TackTabs and Tac' Stik*
- UHU *Tac*

Chapter 7

Pressure Sensitive Adhesives (PSA)

Cellophane tape was introduced in the 1930s as an easy-to-use substitute for string, but before long, people were using it for more than securing the wrappings on packages. Unfortunately, the tape tended to crack and peel away from the adhesive; the adhesive remained on paper and discolored over time. It wasn't until the 1950s that improvements were seen in tapes. The brown stains and bits of tape often found on papers and photos dating from the '30s through the mid-50s are the remains of cellophane tape.

Today, we have a pressure sensitive adhesive (PSA) for just about every surface and purpose. They offer the same "stick and go" feature of that first tape, but we no longer have concerns about the stability of the products. In this chapter, tapes, films, and *Xyron* machines are described. Additional pressure sensitive adhesive products are included in Chapters 8 and 9.

When applying a PSA, it's important that all surfaces are clean, dry, and free of oil and grease. Even the oil from your fingers can affect the performance of these products, so handle the adhesive surface as little as possible.

When cutting a PSA having a liner or release paper with scissors (including decorative edge types), craft knives, rotary cutters, or paper punches, do not remove the liner or paper until after cutting. If the PSA does not have a liner and/or release paper, cover the adhesive with plastic cooking wrap before cutting with scissors, craft knives, or rotary cutters; do not burnish the plastic securely to the adhesive surface. Remove the plastic as soon as cutting is completed. You'll be able to see through the plastic for accurate cutting, and cutting tools (scissors, rotary cutter, craft knives) won't stick to the surfaces being cut. Do not use plastic cooking wrap when using either punches or decorative edge scissors (because it jams the punches and isn't cut by the scissors).

All cutting tools, including punches and decorative edge scissors, can be kept adhesive-free by following this suggestion from Dolly Wood, Specialty Tapes, Inc.: Wipe off the blades with rubbing alcohol, allow to dry, then spray a light coating of a *Silicon* spray over the surface of the blades or the interior of punches. Protect floors when spraying, because *Silicon* is very slippery.

Selecting a PSA is easier if you understand the terms used in connection with them.

ATG (Adhesive Transfer Gun) is a hand-held dispenser used to apply transfer tape. As the adhesive is transferred to a surface, the gun removes the liner on the tape. Some ATGs are designed for very large rolls of transfer tape.

Burnish is to apply pressure with a tool either over the top of the surface to which a PSA has been applied or to the PSA's release paper or liner. Burnishing is often necessary to achieve a bond that is smooth, flat, and secure. Protect the surface being burnished to avoid tears and marks. Vellum is an excellent protector; it's sturdy enough to withstand repeated use, and burnishing tools slide easily on the surface.

De-tacking reduces the tack of an adhesive. Repeatedly place and remove the adhesive side of the PSA on fabric (denim is best) until the tack is reduced. Some, but not all, low tack adhesives can be de-tacked for use as a repositionable (see page 62). Test to determine if the tack is reduced enough for your purposes; thin and fragile papers are easily damaged if too much tack remains.

Double-sided (double-stick) products have an adhesive on each side. A variety of products are double-sided: tapes, including transfer tapes, pre-cut pieces, tapes and pre-cut pieces with a thin layer of foam between the adhesive sides, pre-cut pieces with a thin layer of clear acetate between the adhesive sides, and permanent, repositionable and dual-use films in sizes ranging up to 8-1/2 inches wide.

Dual-use products have a repositionable adhesive on one side and a permanent adhesive on the other. The permanent side is placed on the back of items that will be moved from one surface to another, leaving the repositionable side exposed.

High tack products form a strong, permanent bond. Some instantly bond surfaces together and do not allow for repositioning. That information will be on the label.

Layering is the placement of one or more items on a background. The items often overlap and/or partially cover one another. Layering is a common technique for collage.

Liner is the covering found on transfer tape. It will be colored or clear and plastic or paper. Sometimes the words "release paper," rather than "liner," are used.

Low tack products generally form a repositionable bond on non-porous surfaces, while it is usually permanent on semi-porous and porous surfaces. De-tacking may reduce the adhesive so that it will be repositionable on semi-porous and porous surfaces. Test to ensure results.

Masking is done by placing either a thin, repositionable adhesive film or a masking liquid over a section of a surface to keep a liquid (glue or paint) from that section. The uncut portions of a stencil are a mask and allow you to apply liquid to specific sections through the cut portions of a surface. Rubber stampers use a mask to cover a print when overprinting.

Permanent indicates a bond that is secure and irreversible. Usually there is a cure time before full bond is reached. Permanent does not indicate that the product can be laundered (if it can be, that information will be on the label).

Pressure embossing uses a stencil (often brass) under a layer of paper. A stylus is used to push the paper into the cuts of the stencil, resulting in a raised design on the paper's surface.

Release paper is a non-stick paper found on the adhesive side of many brands of single-faced film. Double-sided film often has a release paper on one side and a liner on the other; the side with the release paper is usually placed on the surface being bonded to another. To easily remove release paper from film, make a small slit in one corner of the paper with an Olfa *Top Layer Paper Cutter*. Lift the paper from the film by sliding your fingernail or the point of a pin into the slit, under the paper. Follow the same procedure to remove a liner.

Repositionable products do not form a permanent bond. They remove easily without residue or damage to a surface. **Always** test when using a repositionable on thin or fragile paper. Some products are repositionable when first applied and allow for repositioning, but then become permanent either after a period of time or when burnished. That information will be on the label.

Self-adhesive (single-stick) products have an adhesive on only one side.

Tack is the degree of bond provided by a product and is described as repositionable, low, or high.

Thermal embossing is the melting of embossing powder with heat using a light bulb, oven, or heat gun (a hair dryer cannot be used). Thick embossing powders (Judi-Kins *Amazing Glaze*, Stewart Superior *Imprintz Enamel*, Suze Weinberg *UTEE*, Therm O Boss *Embossing Enamel*, and Think Ink *Liquid Glass*) are adhesive while still hot (work quickly!). Refer to Chapter 9 for additional information concerning thermal embossing.

Transfer tape is a double-sided tape having a liner on one adhesive side. It is applied either by hand or with a hand-held dispenser. A desktop dispenser rarely is an efficient tool to use with transfer tape. To easily remove the liner from transfer tape applied without a dispenser, first apply the tape to the surface. Burnish the liner (it will be up) to secure the tape on the surface. Make a small slice in the liner and slide the point of a pin into the opening (see release paper above). Lift the liner. Many transfer tapes are packaged in small, refillable, hand-held dispensers. These dispensers, like an ATG, remove the liner as the tape is applied.

Self-adhesive Repositionables

Self-adhesive repositionable products temporarily bond to one surface, temporarily hold one surface on another, and are used for masking and for removable embellishments. Remember to test a repositionable before using it on either paper or untreated wood.

Drafting tape often is used to hold one surface on another; however, liquid (water, paste, glue, paint, etc.) affects the bond of some drafting tapes. If a liquid is involved, test before using this type of tape. Specialty Tapes *Water Color Washout Tape* is not affected by liquids and can be used to secure paper on a nonporous surface when making any of the decorated papers described in Chapters 2, 3 and 5.

Delta *Stencil Mini Repositionable Adhesive Dots* are small, pre-cut circles intended for holding stencils in place; they can be used on most delicate surfaces.

Grafix *Prepared Frisket Film*, a thin vinyl film, is an excellent supply to use when making a mask for rubber stamping. Masks for glued or painted decorative edges and corners can be cut with decorative edge scissors and corner scissors or punches; self-made stencils can be made either with paper punches or die-cut machines. Although the film is thin, it is sturdy, and the masks can be reused several times.

Manco *Removable Easy Liner* removes easily from surfaces, including most papers, and is available in several patterns. *Removable Easy Liner* can be used for self-made stencils. To use paper punches, cover the adhesive side with the shiny side of freezer paper. Slide the layers into the slot of the punch and depress it. The McGill *StrongArm* is a great help when using punches on heavier surfaces.

Most self-adhesive repositionable products also can be used as negative stencils. Rather than placing a liquid into the cut portion of a stencil (a positive stencil), this stencil acts as a mask and will keep the liquid from penetrating the surface where it is placed.

When using a self-adhesive stencil (purchased or self-made), secure the stencil firmly on the surface being stenciled. Do not apply the liquid toward the edges of the stencil. If using a thin liquid, leave the stencil in place until the liquid has dried.

Several advantages are offered when Grafix *Prepared Frisket Film* (Clear or Matte) is used as a mask for rubber stamping. The thin vinyl will not leave a "shadow" line around the overprint, it's leak proof, and the low tack adhesive backing holds the mask securely on the surface when overprinting. Another advantage for the stamper is the easy storage of the mask: it can be placed either on the back of a wooden block over the index or in the storage page for unmounted dies.

To make a rubber stamping mask, print on the film with a permanent dye ink (Clearsnap, Inc. *Ancient Page* is recommended). Holding a heat gun at least 4 inches from the film, apply heat until the print is dry (usually about 45 seconds). Allow to cool. (Note: If desired, the print can air-dry. This will take from one to four hours, depending upon humidity.) Cut out the mask exactly along the outer edges of the print. After printing over the mask, clean ink from the mask with a small piece of cloth.

Stickers and die-cuts labeled "repositionable" remove easily from surfaces. Read the label to determine if the stickers and die-cuts are repositionable; some only are for a short time after application and then cure to a permanent hold.

Double-sided Repositionables

Double-sided repositionable products temporarily bond two surfaces together. Those with either a clear or foam insert between two layers of adhesive also provide height when items are layered on a surface. Dual-use products have a permanent adhesive side and a repositionable adhesive side.

Scotch *ATG Repositionable* and Specialty Tapes *ATG Repositionable* are transfer tapes and can be applied either with an ATG or by hand. Manco *Removable EasyStick*, Moore *Tacky Tape*, Scotch *Repositionable Glue Tape*, and UHU *Multi-Roller Repositionable Adhesive* are available in small hand-held dispensers. Scotch *Wallsaver Removable Poster* is packaged in a disposal desktop dispenser. These products can all be used for temporarily mounting rubber stamp dies on a block, in addition to other uses when a temporary bond is desired.

Manco *Removable Clear Mounting Tabs* and Scotch *Clear Removable Mounting Squares* have a clear insert between two layers of adhesive; Scotch *Wallsaver Removable* has a thin foam layer between two layers of adhesives. These products may not remove easily from thin and fragile papers; test before beginning your project.

Self-adhesive Low Tack

Self-adhesive low tack products generally are not permanent on non-porous surfaces, but usually form a permanent bond on semi-porous and porous surfaces. Most can be de-tacked for use as a repositionable, but always test before use.

Masking tape should not be used with very thin liquids (glues and paints) because they tend to creep under the edges of the tape; however, Tape Systems *White Artist Tape* is not affected by most liquids. Apply liquids away from the edge, rather than toward it. Remove tape as soon as the liquid is dry.

Brands of stencils with an adhesive back include B & B Etching Products, Inc., Delta, and Tulip. The adhesive on these stencils is between a repositionable and a low tack. Blank (uncut) stencil film can be used with paper punches, decorative scissors, corner cutters, and die-cut machines to create your own designs.

B & B Etching Products, Inc. *etchall stencils* can be smoothed flat on surfaces using the *etchall squeegee* shown on page 12. The *Squeegee* also can be used to smooth any brand of stencil, for burnishing, and to apply paste, glue, and paint. In addition to pre-cut designs, blank (uncut) *etchall stencil film* is available; the company also custom cuts stencils using your designs. Test before using these stencils on surfaces other than those that are non-porous; de-tacking may be necessary.

The adhesive on Delta *Monogram Magic, Monogram Magic Sentiments Stencils*, and *Apparel Stencils* can be cleaned and reactivated with soap and water. *Monogram Magic Stencils* are suitable for most surfaces. Although *Apparel Stencils* are intended for clothing, they can be used on other surfaces. Test; de-tacking may be necessary when used on paper.

Tulip *Stick-Easy Stencils* are available in pre-cut designs and blank (uncut) stencil film. Test; de-tacking may be necessary for surfaces other than fabric.

Self-adhesive High Tack

Self-adhesive high tack products form a permanent bond. Some are repositionable when first applied, then cure to a permanent state. The label will contain that information. UnDu Products *un-du* and Ross *De-Solv-it* remove most of these products from surfaces.

Clear and transparent tapes are only some of the many types of self-adhesive products. Laminating film can be used as a protective layer over photos and projects, or as a background surface for a project. Decorative tapes and films quickly add embellishments. Sheets and pre-cut shapes in paper and fabric are available in textures, patterns, and plain varieties. Acrylic beads, craft foam, pressed flowers, rubber stamp mounting supplies, wood appliqués, and wood moldings are available with an adhesive backing. With the exception of acrylic beads and wooden objects, these products can be cut with straight-cut scissors, straight-cut and decorative edge rotary cutters, and craft knives; most can be used in a die-cut machine and with paper punches and template cutting tools.

All of us are familiar with clear and transparent tapes, but here are some that offer different features. Scotch *Document and Photo Mending Tape* and Specialty Tapes *Invisible Mending Tape* are extremely thin and can be used for mending magazine and book pages. Manco *OneTouch Invisible Tape* is packaged in a small, refillable hand applicator that allows you to apply tape with one hand. Scotch *Pop-up Magic Tape Strips* are pre-cut 2-inch strips used in the handy *Pop-up Dispenser*. Manco *Clear Polyethylene Weatherseal Tape* is very sturdy and bonds well to smooth, slick surfaces.

Clear and textured laminating films are available in a variety of weights. Grafix *Heavy-Weight Laminating Film* is a heat-resistant *Mylar* and can be thermal embossed, while Grafix *Light-Weight Laminating Film* has a gridded release paper to aid in placement. Manco *Clear Transparent Easy Stick Liner* is thin and sturdy. Therm O Web *PeelnStick Acid-Free Decorative Laminating Sheets* are available in matte and gloss finishes and leather and linen textures, while *Keep A Memory Acid-Free Laminates* are available in matte and gloss finishes.

In addition to tapes and laminating films, a wide variety of high tack self-adhesive products are available, and the number continues to grow.

Paper Adventures *Paper Applique* and *Create-your-own Stickers & Seals* (available in three styles) can be decorated before being bonded to a surface. Stampers find these prod-

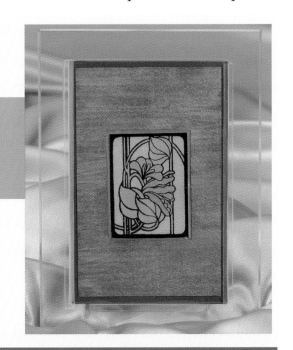

Project

Framed Stained Glass Stamp Print

The white tissue paper used for this print allows the light to show through the back of the print when placed in a clear frame.

You Will Need

Stained glass stamp: Stamp from Stained Glass Plate (42-S) ©NonSequitur Rubberstamps (used in example)
1/4 sheet white tissue paper
Genesis *Artist Colors*: Black
Genesis *Artist Colors Thinning Medium*
Darice *Embossing Essentials Foam Daubers*
Stewart Superior *Imprintz Clear Detail Embossing Powder*
Clearsnap Detail Embossing Powder: Clear
Grafix *Heavy-Weight Laminating Film*
1/4-inch wide double-sided tape
Gum arabic colored with dye re-inkers (blending with powdered mica pigments optional)
Small brush
1/4-inch foil tape: Gold
Colored mat board (size needed to fit in frame)

Decorated paper, purchased or self-made (self-made paste paper was used in the example; it was cut 1/2 inch shorter and 1/2 inch narrower than the mat board)
Clear glass frame*
Optional: rotary cutter, mat and ruler or Fiskars *Paper Trimmer*
Miscellaneous supplies: scissors, iron, cooking parchment paper or *Teflon* pressing sheet, scrap piece of vellum larger than the stamp print, burnishing tool, *Fine-Line Air Erasable Marker* from Clotilde, stylus, craft knife, small glass plate, craft stick, non-stick work surface for blending re-inkers and powdered mica pigments to color the print

*The print can be placed on a Prairie Stamper *Acrylic Block* rather than a glass frame as shown in the example.

1. Cut a piece of tissue paper that is 2 inches wider and longer than the stamp print; cut a piece of the *Laminating Film* to the same size. Set the *Laminating Film* aside.

2. Cover the tissue paper with either cooking parchment paper or a *Teflon* pressing sheet. Set the iron at medium heat and press the tissue paper smooth and flat. Allow to cool.

3. Place approximately 1/4 teaspoon of the black *Genesis Artist Colors* on the glass plate; blend 1/8 teaspoon of the *Thinning Medium* into the black. Tap the foam dauber in the paint. The foam should be evenly covered with the *Genesis Artist Colors*. Place the stamp on a flat surface with the die up. Tap the inked dauber over the die. The coating of the paint on the die should be even and cover all raised areas of the die. Re-ink the dauber as necessary.

4. Print the image in the center of the tissue paper. Sprinkle the clear embossing powder over the print. Shake off excess embossing powder. Aiming the gun at the center of the print, heat the powder until it has melted; powder along the edges will melt as the center melts.

5. Remove the release paper from the *Laminating Film*. Place the film on the back of the tissue paper (the side that is not embossed). Burnish lightly to secure the film to the tissue. Set aside.

6. Blend the re-inkers and powdered mica pigments to reach the desired colors (three colors were used in the sample). Using the small brush, color the print on the front, within the embossed areas. In the example, the larger areas surrounding the flower were not colored. Allow to dry.

7. Cut the decorated paper to the needed size (see You Will Need). Place the foil tape along each outer edge of the front of the embossed print. Place the decorated paper, back up, on a flat surface. Place the print, embossed side down, in the center of the decorated paper. Run a small stylus around the outer edges of the gold foil tape to score the decorated paper. Remove the print.

8. Use a craft knife to cut along the scored line. Remove the cut portion from the center of the decorated paper. Place the embossed print behind the opening. If the opening is larger than the outer edges of the foil tape on the print, add another band of tape next to the first. Remove the print.

9. Place the mat board, front up, on a flat surface. Place the decorated paper, front up, on the mat board. Using the *Fine-Line Air Erasable Marker*, trace the opening cut in the decorated paper on the mat board. Remove the decorated paper and cut the opening in the mat board with a craft knife.

10. With the decorated paper face down on a flat surface, place a strip of the 1/4-inch adhesive tape along each side of the opening. Remove the release paper from the tape. Position the embossed print, face down, over the tape. Cover the taped areas with vellum and burnish to secure. Remove the vellum.

11. Leaving the decorated paper face down, place a strip of the 1/4-inch tape along each of the outer edges of the decorated paper. Place the mat board over the decorated paper, lining up the openings cut in the decorated paper and mat board. Cover the mat board with vellum and burnish. Remove the vellum.

12. Slide the finished print into the channels on the front of the frame.

13. Optional: Rather than using a glass frame, the print can be mounted to the front of an acrylic block. Cover the back of the mat board with a double-sided adhesive film and position the print on the front of the block. Cover with vellum and lightly burnish to secure the bond.

ucts a useful supply for layered backgrounds, and also for prints they cut out to bond to a card. They are an easy supply to use for creating self-made borders and designs for scrapbook pages.

Bemiss-Jason *Glitter Dots* are permanent on most surfaces and can be used on clothing (remove before laundering). ColArt Americas *Glass Tile & Metal Works Foil Tape* is available in silver, gold, bronze, and copper. Grafix *Funky Film* is available in a wide range of designs and patterns; Grafix *Funky Tape* is the same plastic film as *Funky Film* and is available in many of the same patterns. The high tack backing on Magnaproducts *Make-a-Magnet* sheets, pre-cut shapes, and tape is suitable for many surfaces. Manco *Aluminum Foil Tape* is a shiny silver tape that can be pressure embossed, thermal embossed, antiqued with craft paint, or cut into thin strips. Plaid *Gallery Glass Redi-Lead* can be used on surfaces other than glass. Tower Hobbys *Trim Tapes* are available in a wide variety of widths (including 1/16-inch) and colors. Generally used on model cars and planes, they can be used on just about every surface.

Beadery *Hair Jazz Clip Kits* contain all of the supplies needed to quickly make decorated hair clips with acrylic beads. One of the designs available is shown below.

Cache Junction *Sticky-Back Velvet Paper* can be heat embossed with rubber stamps, and *Clip 'n Stick Paper Piecing Kits* are available in several designs. Pamela Shoy *Create-A-Border* and *Create-A-Quilt* are pre-cut paper shapes.

Dritz offers adhesive felt alphabets and numbers. Kunin *Presto Felt* is available in dots, alphabets, and numbers. Grafix *Funky Fur* is a washable fabric. Papershops *Cotton Fabric,* cotton calico sheets in a variety of patterns, are a handy decorating supply for doll houses.

NuCentury *Real Flower Pages* and *Fabulous Frames* are laminated pressed flowers; they can be used as stickers or on photo mats or scrapbook pages.

Artistic Wood *Wood Appliqués* and *Wood Moldings* are pre-sanded, primed, and ready for painting or staining. The example seen above was painted with craft paint and antiqued with Craf-T Products Gold *Metallic Rub-Ons.* The same supplies were used for the Dritz *Tassel Topper* placed on the Tassel Of Many Colors, made using Sueperstuff Fibers, shown above.

Darice *"Sticky" Back Foamies* are an excellent supply to use for many crafting activities. In addition to using cut or punched pieces as embellishments, the craft foam is ideal for making your own stamps. Two other self-adhesive products of interest to those who enjoy making their own stamps are Dharma Trading *Flexi-Stamp* and Jim Stephan *Quickie Mounts.*

To quickly make stamps using either *Flexi-Stamp* from Dharma Trading or Darice *"Sticky" Back Foamies*, have the foam side up for both shapes and cut out two identical shapes (large or giant paper punches, traced cookie cutters, your design, etc.). Remove the release paper from one shape. To make the stamp, place the adhesive side of the first shape on the foam side of the second shape.

Cut a piece of 6mm Darice *Foamies* slightly larger than the shape to use as the block for the stamp. (If a thicker block is desired, use Jim Stephan *Quickie Mount*; see below.) Remove the release paper from the back of the second shape and press the shapes onto the block. Ink with a regular stamp pad. When finished stamping, remove the ink from the "stamp" with a damp cloth. A reverse stamp can be made by having the release paper up when making the two shapes.

Quickie Mount is a dense, firm foam intended for a block when mounting rubber and polymer stamps; it's also an excellent block for all types of sponge stamps. A mounted sponge (including expanded-sponge) stamp produces a better print when mounted; the block also keeps your hands clean. Easily cut with a craft knife, *Quickie Mount* also is an easy-to-use supply when carving stamps. Cut into strips, the foam can be used for applying glue, paint, or stamping ink to surfaces. Wipe off wet glue, paint, or ink with a damp cloth.

Technique

Decorated Pen

A product not generally thought of as a general crafts supply is Sulky *Self-Adhesive Stabilizer*. The stabilizer can be decorated with craft paints (including fabric paint), markers, and embossing powders prior to being placed on just about every porous and non-porous surface. Further, Really, Really Faux Paste Paper (on page 48) and stickers are quickly made with the stabilizer.

It's an excellent supply to use for covering pens; the stabilizer allows for secure placement of many embellishments that do not bond well to a pen's plastic barrel.

1. To cover a pen barrel, cut a piece of the stabilizer (either decorated or plain) that is 1 inch wider than the circumference and 1 inch longer than the length of the pen (from pen point to end). Place the pen in the center of the stabilizer piece, having an extension of 1/2 inch at each end. Bring the two long edges of the stabilizer up over the barrel. Smooth the stabilizer on the barrel and press the two adhesive sides of the stabilizer together. Run your fingernail down the side of the barrel to secure the two adhesive sides tightly together.

2. Using scissors, cut the two layers of stabilizer close to, but not directly on, the crease. Burnish the cut edge with the back of your thumbnail. The junction where the two adhesive sides of the stabilizer were joined will hardly be visible.

3. Tightly twist the extension at the end of the pen and clip off the excess next to the end of the pen. If desired, glue or dimensional fabric paint can be placed on the twisted area and adorned with plastic jewels, small beads, glitter, etc.

4. Place the blade of a craft knife in the area where the barrel joins the area above the tip of the pen. Holding the blade stable, roll the pen to cut away the excess stabilizer. Twist the pen between your thumb and index finger to secure the stabilizer to the pen.

Project

Polymer Clay Magnet

This magnet is large enough to hold items securely to the front of the refrigerator—it puts an end to the slip-sliding problem presented by smaller magnets.

You Will Need

5- x 8-inch sheet of Magnaproducts *Make-a-Magnet*

Translucent *Sculpey III Polymer Clay*

Small roller for clay (i.e. a piece of PVC pipe, glass, etc.)

Embossing ink or glycerin for preparing the cookie press

Clay cookie press

Acrylic craft paint: Red, gold, and black

Polyform *Sculpey Glaze* in Matte

Miscellaneous supplies: cotton swabs, craft knife, small paintbrush, disposable paint palette, small sponge, fine grit sand paper or emery board, rubbing alcohol, scissors

1. After conditioning the clay thoroughly per the manufacturer's instructions, roll it out to a 1/2-inch thickness. Dip a cotton swab in the embossing ink or glycerin and coat all surfaces of the front of the cookie press with the liquid. If any of the liquid pools in the press, dab it out with a clean swab.

2. Place the cookie press on a flat surface and place the clay over it. Using your fingertips, push the clay into the press, adding more clay so the back of the clay is flat.

3. Turn over; the clay will be down. Use the craft knife to cut away excess clay from around the edges of the press. Leaving the clay in the press, bake at the temperature and for the amount of time listed on the clay's package. Bake with the clay up. Allow to cool. Remove the clay from the press.

4. Using the brush, apply *Sculpey Glaze* to the front of the clay. Allow to dry. Apply the glaze to the back. When dry, apply a second coat of glaze to the back. Allow to dry.

5. Add small amounts of the craft paints to the palette. Dip the end of the sponge in the red and apply to the front of the clay. When dry, apply black to the recessed areas with the sponge; use the sponge to wipe off excess black. Allow to dry. Apply gold with the sponge over the raised portions of the design and around the edges, rubbing off some of the paint to accent portions of the design. Allow to dry. Apply *Sculpey Glaze* over the front of the clay; allow to dry.

6. Lightly sand the back of the clay; wipe off the sanded area with rubbing alcohol. Allow to dry. Place the adhesive side of the magnetic sheet on the back of the clay. Trim away excess.

Polymer clay medallions also can be used as embellishments for trinket boxes, like the two shown here. One medallion was made using a clay cookie press. The other was made by pressing clay into a candy mold; in this case, the clay was removed from the mold before curing (baking). A double-sided, high tack adhesive film was applied to the back of the medallion after the second coat of glaze was applied and sanded. Excess film was cut away along the edges of the medallion. The medallion was positioned on the lid of a painted paper maché box and pressure was applied to secure the medallion to the lid.

Double-sided High Tack

Double-sided high tack adhesive products can be used either for bonding surfaces together or to bond embellishments to a surface. With few exceptions, these products bond well to all surfaces. Some are repositionable until burnished; that information will be on the label. Although labeled "permanent," do not use on fabric that will be laundered unless the label indicates that option.

Most can be used to bond almost every type of embellishment, including powdered pigments, craft foil, acrylic beads, metal leaf, glass beads and no-hole beads, small charms, shrink plastic, glitter, and Signature Crafts *Glitter Silvers*. Several are suitable to use with embossing powder and can be thermal embossed. To ensure success, test before beginning your project.

Many of the following brands of double-sided and transfer tapes are packaged in a refillable dispenser. Tapes on larger cores can be applied either by hand or in an ATG. Tapes suitable for thermal embossing are noted.

- 3L *Photo Tape* (can be thermal embossed)
- Art Accents *Tacky Tape* (can be thermal embossed)
- Darice *Embossing Essentials* (available in four widths; can be thermal embossed
- Dritz *Double-Faced Sewing/Craft Tape* (available in three widths; can be thermal embossed)
- *bama TapeRoller* from Making Memories (can be thermal embossed)
- Judi-Kins *Mosaic Tape* (can be thermal embossed)
- Manco Plastic *Indoor/Outdoor Carpet Tape* (this product forms a very strong bond that is waterproof), *All Purpose Carpet Tape*, and *Easy-Stick* (this product can be thermal embossed)
- Pioneer *Photo Memory Mounting Tape*
- Scotch *Double-Stick Adhesive Pen, Glue Tape*, and *Photo & Document Mounting Tape*
- Specialty Tapes *Stitchery Tape* and *D993/Double Length* (both can be thermal embossed)
- Sunday International *Great Tape* (can be thermal embossed)
- Suze Weinberg *Wonder Tape* (available in four widths; can be thermal embossed)
- Therm o Web *PeelNStick Double Sided Adhesive* and *Keep A Memory Mounting Tape* (both can be thermal embossed)
- TSI/Tape Systems Inc. *Heat Embossable Tape* (available in four widths; can be thermal embossed)
- UHU *Multi-Roller Permanent* (can be thermal embossed)
- USArtQuest *Ah, That's Great Tape* (can be thermal embossed)

Double-sided tapes with a thin layer of foam between two adhesives include Manco *Tape for Mounting* and Scotch *Mounting Tape*.

Many transfer tapes are packaged in a refillable dispenser. Those on a larger core can be used either in an ATG or applied by hand. All mentioned transfer tapes can be thermal embossed.

Double-sided, pre-cut shapes include:
- 3L *PhotoFix Mounting Squares* (can be thermal embossed)
- Aleene's *Instant Fix-It Strips* (3- x 1-inch strips, can be thermal embossed)
- National Artcraft *Ultra Thin Sticky Dots*
- Scratch-Art *3 D-O'S* (small circles with a layer of 1/4-inch thick foam between two adhesives) and *Paste Mates* (can be thermal embossed)

- Specialty Tapes *Master Tabs II*
- Tape Systems *Heat Embossing Dots* and *Heavy Duty Beadable Scallop/Wave Tape* (both products can be thermal embossed)
- Therm O Web *Instant Solutions Replacement Tape* (2-1/4- x 3-inch pieces, can be thermal embossed)
- UHU *fix Mounting Tabs* (small rectangles with a layer of 1/8-inch thick foam between two adhesives)

Bainbridge *Craft Tac* and Therm O Web *Keep A Memory Acid-Free Sticky Dots Adhesive Sheets* are a series of small adhesive dots on a release paper. After the adhesive is applied to the back of an item (follow the manufacturer's directions), it is not necessary to cut away excess; adhesive lingering along the edges is rubbed off with your finger or an eraser used for rubber cement. This type of adhesive is extremely useful for bonding irregular shaped items and designs to paper (punched shapes, die-cuts, paper and fabric lace, fibers, Ogura lace paper, acrylic jewels, etc.). Both can be thermal embossed. *Sticky Dots* are suitable for use on non-porous surfaces and surfaces that present bonding problems (i.e., candles). *Sticky Dots* are available in two sizes of sheets and 1/4-inch tape. *Craft Tac* is available in two sizes of sheets and is repositionable for up to 24 hours.

Project
Foiled Candle

Fast, easy, safe to burn, and eye-catching—this candle has it all!

You Will Need

Candle
Rubbing alcohol and paper towels or
  packaged alcohol swabs
Therm O Web *Keep A Memory Acid-Free
Sticky Dots Adhesive*
Sunday International Multi-Color *Craft Foil*

---

1. Wipe off all of the candle's surfaces with rubbing alcohol. Allow to dry.

2. Lift the release paper covering the *Sticky Dots Adhesive*. Holding the candle by the ends, roll it over the adhesive until the surface of the candle is covered with the adhesive. Depending on the coverage desired, it may be necessary to reposition the candle on the sheet of adhesive and roll again one or two more times.

3. Wrap the foil around the candle with the dull side of the foil down. Use your fingers to burnish the foil to the adhesive.

4. Remove the foil. If any areas of the

adhesive are not covered with foil, place the dull side of the foil on those areas and burnish with your fingertip.

Note: To apply plastic jewels to the candle, place the jewels, back down, on the adhesive. Cover with the release paper and burnish the tops of the jewels with your fingertip. Lift the release paper, pick up the jewels (a tweezers is helpful for picking up smaller jewels), position them on the candle, and press in place with the your fingertip.

Double-sided Sheets

Double-sided sheets, either uncut or cut, provide instant decoration with a variety of crafting supplies, including small beads, small plastic jewels, powdered mica pigments, and small dried flowers. Most sheets can be thermal embossed, allowing for the use of embossing powder.

These sheets can be used in sheet form, cut into strips with a rotary cutter, cut with scissors (plain cut and decorative edge), and used in paper punches. When cutting or punching paper to which it has been supplied, leave the release paper in place until cutting and/or punching is completed.

> **Double-sided sheet products include:**
> - Darice *Embossing Essentials*
> - Tape Systems *Heavy Duty Heat Embossing Beadable Sheets*
> - Therm O Web *PeelnStick Double Sided Adhesive*, *Keep A Memory Acid-Free Mounting Adhesive*, and *Keep A Memory Acid-Free Sticky Dots Adhesive*
>
> **All of these can be thermal embossed.**

Project

Instant Paper Beads

Thanks to double-sided adhesive sheets, these beads are made in a snap—provided you don't get too involved in the fun of decorating them.

> ### You Will Need
> High tack double-sided sheets
> Scrap pieces of vellum in various colors and patterns
> Dritz *Children's Plastic Sewing Needle*
> Pigment ink
> Rotary cutter, ruler, and cutting mat
> Optional decorating supplies: colored wire, foil tape, embroidery floss

1. Cover one side of each piece of vellum with an adhesive sheet. Using the rotary cutter, cut strips that are 1-3/4 inches wide and up to 3 inches long. Wipe the pointed end of the needle across a pigment ink stamp pad. This must be done each time the needle is used for making beads.

2. Place a vellum strip on a flat surface, adhesive side up. Remove the release paper from the adhesive. Place the needle across the 1-3/4-inch width, 1/4 inch from the end. Press the needle on the adhesive.

3. Bring the cut end of the strip up over the needle and press it to the adhesive on the other side of the needle. Begin rolling the vellum on the needle, keeping the outer edges as even as possible. Continue rolling to the end of the strip. Use the back of your thumbnail to secure the end of the strip to the top of the bead. Slide the bead off the needle.

4. If the ends of the bead are not even, place the bead on the rotary cutting mat and press the cutter through the end of the bead to remove the uneven end.

5. Decorating the beads is optional, but it's a lot of fun. Wrap embroidery floss, colored wire, or foil tape around the beads, as desired.

Project

Asian Collage

The time required to create a collage card is greatly reduced when all bonding is done with a double-sided adhesive. This example includes both porous and non-porous surfaces, all of which were easily bonded.

You Will Need

Art Accents *Collage Elements*, Geisha Collection
Friendly Plastic: Red
Thick Ink *Liquid Glass*: Gold
Rubber Stamp ©Clearsnap Spiral
Clearsnap *Top Boss Embossing Ink Pad*
Origami paper: Black
One piece of faux marble transparency film (refer to Faux Marble Book Mark, page 75)
Art Accents *Art Boardz* in the color of your choice
Darice *Embossing Essentials Adhesive Film*
Heat gun
Miscellaneous supplies: scissors, plastic cook wrap, piece of scrap vellum slightly larger than the mat board, burnishing tool
Optional: Rotary cutter, ruler, cutting mat

Note: Cutting can be done either with scissors or rotary cutting tools. Follow the method described in Step 1 when trimming excess adhesive from all supplies; do not remove the release paper from the back of the adhesive until after the design of the collage has been determined (Step 5). Purchased or self-made decorative paper can be substituted for the faux marble transparency film, if desired.

1. Cut out the Geisha print from the *Collage Elements* sheet. Place *Adhesive Film* on the back of the print. Cover the front of the print with plastic cooking wrap and trim the film to the edges of the print. Set aside.

2. Cut a 2-inch long piece of *Friendly Plastic*. Cover the back with the *Adhesive Film*. Trim the adhesive to the edges of the plastic. Using the heat gun, heat the plastic until it is soft and a little sticky. Sprinkle a small amount of the gold *Liquid Glass* powder over the soft plastic; the surface should not be covered with the powder. Press the powder into the surface of the plastic with the tip of your finger. Ink the stamp with the embossing ink.

3. Heat the plastic until the embossing powder melts; immediately press the inked stamp into the plastic. Only a portion of the stamp will print due to the size of the plastic. Allow to cool. Remove the stamp.

4. Place adhesive on the back of the faux marble transparency film and origami paper; trim to the edges. Arrange the collage design on the front of the *Art Boardz*. Cut the transparency film and origami paper in the sizes needed for the design.

5. When pleased with the design, remove the release paper from the adhesive on the origami paper; position it on the mat board. Cover with vellum and burnish. Add the transparency film in the same manner. Remove the release paper from the back of the *Friendly Plastic* and position it on the origami paper. Press firmly with your fingertip to secure it to the paper. Remove the release paper from the back of the Geisha print. Position in place and burnish.

Faux Marble Bookmark

This is messy to make, but the results make it worthwhile. Like Paste Paper (see page 21), every piece made can be used, either as a full piece or cut into shapes and designs for embellishing paper crafts.

You Will Need

Clear transparency film for laser printer
ZimInk Permanent: Black, silver, and
  gold
Rubbing alcohol
Scratch-Art *Lolli-Foam Brush*
1/4 sheet of double-sided adhesive
Bookmark tassel
Miscellaneous supplies: scissors, small
  disposable aluminum cake pan, paper
  towels, piece of scrap vellum slightly
  larger than the size of the finished
  bookmark, burnishing tool, hole
  punch
Optional: Disposable plastic gloves,
  rotary cutter, ruler, cutting mat
Note: Cutting can be done with either
scissors or rotary tools.

---

1. Line the bottom of the cake pan with four thicknesses of paper towels. Cut the sheet of transparency film in half and place it in the pan; the film should lie flat. Add a quarter cup of alcohol to the pan.
2. Shake the bottles of ink well. Drop small amounts of the black ink randomly on the film; the drops should be no more than 1/4 inch across and spaced 1/2 inch apart. Drop small amounts of the silver ink between the black ink. Dip the corner of the foam brush into the rubbing alcohol and shake the alcohol over the film. This will cause the ink to blend and run over the surface of the film.
3. Immediately drop small amounts of the gold ink over the still-wet ink on the film. Dip the corner of the foam brush into the alcohol; if alcohol is dripping from the brush, squeeze it slightly against the side of the pan. Twist the rounded edge of the foam brush on the inked surface of the film to blend the three colors of ink. Set aside to dry.
4. Remove the film from the pan and hold it up to the light. If there are areas on the film that do not have ink, apply drops of gold ink to those areas. Dip the foam brush into the alcohol, squeeze out any excess, and twist the rounded end of the brush over the gold. Allow to dry.
5. Place the double-sided adhesive over the back of the transparency film. Place a plain piece of transparency film on the adhesive. With the back up, cover with vellum and burnish. Trim to the size desired for the bookmark. Punch a hole in the center top of the bookmark and add the tassel.

Laminating

Xyron introduced a cold (non-electric) laminating machine in the mid-1990s. It was specifically designed for crafting and was an instant success. Now available in four sizes to handle widths of 1/12, 5, 8-1/2 and 12 inches, each can be used with items not exceeding a thickness of 1/10 inch (2.5mm).

Depending on the cartridge and machine, items are quickly and easily laminated on one or both sides, laminated on one side with an adhesive on the other, have an adhesive placed on one side, or have a magnetic sheet placed on one side. Adhesive cartridges are available in repositionable, acid-free, low tack, and high tack.

As you turn the handle, the rollers in the machine securely and evenly apply the adhesive, laminating, or magnetic layer; burnishing is not required. The built-in cutter removes the item from the machine. No wonder *Xyron* was an instant success!

Chapter 9 includes several suggested uses for *Xyron* cartridges for scrapbooking, including making your own stickers, mounting photos, and layering papers. These techniques should not be limited to scrapbooking; they are suitable for all paper crafting activities.

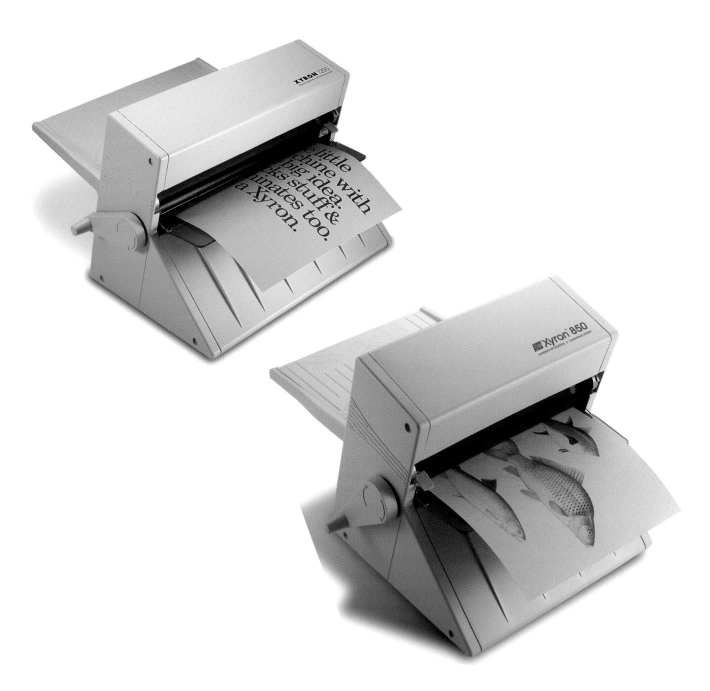

Another use for the 8-1/2- and 12-inch wide machines does not involve using a cartridge (it must be removed from the machine). Soft clays, including conditioned polymer clays, can be rolled through the rollers resulting in a smooth, even piece of clay that will be approximately 3mm thick.

1. Cut a piece of freezer paper that is at least 12 inches long and 1 inch narrower than the width of the rollers. Fold the 12-inch length in half with the shiny sides together. Roll the clay into a ball. Use your palm to flatten the ball to a 1/2-inch thickness. Open the freezer paper and place the flattened clay in the center of one 6-inch half of the folded sheet. The outer edges of the clay must be a minimum of 2 inches from each side of the freezer paper. Bring the other half of the freezer paper over the clay; it must be completely covered with the freezer paper.

2. Place the folded edge of the paper just between the two rollers. Roll the paper/clay through the machine in a continuous roll forward and then back (stopping and starting the motion will result in "wavy" surface on the top of the clay). If desired, the clay can be left on the freezer paper for shaping, cutting, stamping and/or air drying. Polymer clay can be left on the paper for curing in the oven; remove from the paper when cool.

Chapter 8

Acid-free, pH Neutral, and Archival Glues and Adhesives

The products described in this chapter are labeled by the manufacturer as acid-free, pH neutral (7.0), and/or archival, making them suitable for use with photographs, in photo albums and scrapbooks, and for memorabilia, but they are not limited to these uses. They provide excellent bonding and can be used for many crafting activities (for example Aleene's *Memory Glue* is an excellent adhesive for craft foam, while TomBow *Colored Glue Stick* and *Clear Glue Stick* are favored by many for vellum). Liquid repositionable adhesives can be used for projects containing craft foil, metal leaf, glitter and small, no-hole beads, and pressure sensitive adhesives can be used with several crafting supplies and for several techniques.

In general, these adhesive products will not, over time, cause damage either to photos or memorabilia. Depending on the product, the bond will be either water-reversible or permanent.

Water-reversible and Permanent

Water-reversible products are easily removed with water after drying. For many, this is the only type of adhesive considered when mounting photographs or memorabilia; however, some of these products can be affected by humidity and dampness, which could affect the bond over time. Most are not UV-resistant. Included in this category are natural adhesives, synthetic adhesives, and glue sticks.

Permanent products require the use of a remover, usually solvent-based, for complete removal after drying. The long-term permanency offered by these adhesives is an important feature for many. Rarely are they affected by humidity, and several are UV-resistant. Included

in this category are acrylic-based adhesives, synthetic adhesives, repositionable adhesives, pressure sensitive adhesives, spray adhesives, hot glues, and solvent-based adhesives.

Application

Application methods for water-reversible and permanent adhesives are determined by the type of the adhesive.

With the exception of pressure sensitive adhesives, remember **less is best** when applying adhesives. Too thick an application often results in the adhesive either seeping or soaking through one or both of the surfaces. The bond often is not increased by a thick coat; in fact, it may be diminished. Test the product you have selected to determine the amount needed for a secure bond on the surfaces involved.

In most cases, burnishing is necessary to secure the bond. Photographs and fragile items should be covered before burnishing. You can place a "reject" photograph (a less than perfect one) print side down over photographs, cover flat items (papers, stickers, etc) with acid-free vellum (two brands are Bemiss-Jason and Paper Adventures), or wrap white acid-free tissue paper, folded four layers thick, over your fingertip to burnish items that have a textured or raised surface. Burnishing tools include the Clover Needlecraft, Inc. *Finger Presser* and Scratch Art *Rubbing Stick* and *Soft Rubber Brayer*.

After removing the excess adhesive, pick up the item and position it on the surface to which it is being bonded. Cover the item with one of the supplies suggested on the previous page before burnishing. Beginning at the center and moving out to the edges, gently smooth the item flat.

Pick up the covering from the item. If any adhesive has seeped from under the edges of the item, wipe it off with a slightly damp cotton swab or blot it with white tissue paper. Replace the covering, making sure the side covering the item is adhesive-free. Burnish the edges again to secure the bond. Remove the covering; allow the adhesive to dry.

When working with larger items, consider using the Come Quilt With Me *Brooklyn Revolver* described in Chapter 1. Remember to completely cover the top of the *Brooklyn Revolver* with plastic cooking wrap or a plastic shower cap before beginning. Use of the *Revolver* is not recommended with either hot glues or solvent-based adhesives.

Glue Sticks

Glue sticks should be applied in a thin, even coat directly from the tube. In general, glue sticks are better suited for bonding lightweight or smaller items. Place the item, face down, on a stack of paper or a phone book (see page 9). Apply the glue stick either along the edges or to the entire back (most manufacturers recommend covering the entire back). Unless a thick coat is applied, it will not be necessary to remove the excess adhesive. Position the item on the surface, cover the item with vellum or cooking parchment paper, and burnish as directed for liquid adhesives. (See Chapter 4 for more on glue sticks.)

Liquid Repositionable Adhesives

Liquid repositionable adhesives are packaged in applicator bottles, rolling ball pens, and markers. Many of these adhesives offer the option of being used as either a permanent or a repositionable (temporary) bond. The label will have that information.

When used for a permanent bond, apply from the container in a thin coat. Those in rolling ball pens and markers tend to dry quickly; when used with larger items, apply only to the edges. Burnish as directed for liquid adhesives (see page 19).

When used for a repositionable bond, apply in a thin coat. Leaving the item face down, allow the adhesive to dry to a tacky state. Most of these adhesives change color when dry, and some dry clear. After the adhesive has dried, the item can be placed on a surface and removed from that surface as desired. Do not burnish.

Brands of liquid repositionable adhesives include:
- **Crafter's Pick** *Craqueleur Base Coat*
- **Fiskars** *Photo Memories Glue Pen*
- **Frances Meyer, Inc.** *Memories 2-in-1 Glue Marker* and *2-in-1 Glue Pen*
- **Leeho** *2 in 1 Glue Marker* by **Sailor** and **Sailor** *Rolling Ball 2 in 1 Glue Pen* (available in two tip sizes)
- **Paper Adventures** *Archival Glue*
- **Sunday International** *Foil Magic*
- **Tombow** *MonoMulti Liquid Glue*
- **USArtQuest** *Duo Embellishing Adhesive* (can be applied from the bottle, with a brush, or a USArtQuest *Fine Liner Pen*)
- **Zig** *Memory System 2 Way Glue*

Pressure Sensitive Adhesives

Pressure sensitive adhesives are either double-sided (double-stick) or self-adhesive (single-sided). Double-sided products include film, adhesive dots, tape, pre-cut mounting pieces, and *Xyron* cartridges. Self-adhesive products include photo corners, mounting corners, stickers, die-cuts, embellishments, mending tape, laminating film, and *Xyron* cartridges. All of these products form an instant bond, although many allow for repositioning of items either for a period following application or before being burnished. The label will have that information.

The product determines where the adhesive is placed on the item: double-sided film, tape, adhesive dots, pre-cut mounting pieces, and *Xyron* adhesive film are placed on the back, while photo corners, mounting corners, self-adhesive stickers, adhesive die-cuts, embellishments, and laminating film (including *Xyron*) are placed on the front; self-adhesive tape intended for repair and mending is placed on the back.

UnDu Products *un-du* removes pressure sensitive adhesives without damage to photographs. Read and follow the manufacturer's directions and always test.

Avoid touching the adhesive layer when working. The oils in your skin affect the tack of the adhesive.

Double-sided Film

Double-sided film has a release paper covering each side of the adhesive. Place the item receiving the adhesive face down on a non-stick surface. Remove the release paper from one side of the adhesive and apply to the back of the item.

Trim away excess film from curved edges with scissors. When trimming away excess film from straight edges, either a rotary cutter or paper cutter is faster than scissors. Two methods for keeping scissors blades, rotary cutter blades, and paper cutter blades free from sticky residue are described on page 60.

After trimming away the excess, remove the release paper from the back of the film and position the item on the surface to which it is being bonded. When the item is correctly positioned, burnish following the directions given at the beginning of this chapter.

If a *Xyron* machine is used to apply the

adhesive film, place the item face up on the tray. Leave the clear cover and release paper in place when the item is removed from the machine. Trim away excess adhesive. Remove the release paper (the clear cover will fall way as you trim) and position the item on the surface to which it is being bonded. When the item is correctly positioned, cover it with a protective surface and burnish to secure the bond.

Bainbridge *Craft Tac* and Therm O Web *Keep A Memory Acid-Free Sticky Dots* do not require cutting away excess adhesive after being applied, regardless of an item's shape. After applying either of these adhesives to the back of the item, remove any adhesive extending beyond the edges with either your fingertip or an eraser used to remove rubber cement. Position the item on the surface to which it is being bonded; cover your fingertip with tissue paper and lightly burnish the item. Both products can be thermal embossed. *Craft Tac* is repositionable for up to 24 hours and is available in two sizes of sheets; *Sticky Dots* is available in tape and sheets.

Double-sided Tape, Transfer Tape, and Mounting Pieces

Double-sided tape, transfer tape, and mounting pieces are used when either the size or weight of an item does not require you to apply an adhesive to its entire back for secure bonding. Tape is applied either to each corner or along the outer edges of an item, while mounting pieces generally are applied only to each corner.

Transfer tape differs from regular double-sided tape in that it has a release covering on one side. Transfer tape can be applied either by hand or with an ATG dispenser (see page 60). When transfer tape is applied by hand, the release covering is removed after the tape has been applied to the first surface.

Place the item receiving the adhesive face down on a non-stick surface; apply the adhesive either to each corner or along the edges of the item. Line up the edge of the tape or mounting piece along the outside edge of the item. When the item is correctly positioned on the surface to which it is being bonded, burnish following the directions given at the beginning of this chapter.

In addition to *Xyron, Keep A Memory Acid-Free Sticky Dots Adhesive*, and Bainbridge *Craft Tac*, brands of double-sided adhesive film include:
- Darice *Embossing Essentials Adhesive Film* and *Embossing Essentials Double-sided Adhesive Film*
- Grafix *Double Stick' N Stay* and *Double Tack*
- Suze Weinberg *Wonder Sheets*
- Therm O Web *Keep A Memory Acid-Free Mounting Adhesive*
- TSI/Tape Systems, Inc. *Heavy Duty Embossable Film*

Brands of double-sided and transfer tape include:
- 3L *PhotoTape*
- Art Accents *Tacky Tape*
- Darice *Embossing Essentials Double-sided Tape*
- *hama Taperoller* from Making Memories (Note: This tape is in segments and can be applied from the dispenser either as a continuous piece or in small pieces.)
- Judi-Kins *Mosaic Double Stick Tape*
- Manco *Easy Stick*
- Pioneer *Album Mounting Tape*
- Scotch *Double-Stick Adhesive Pen, Permanent Glue Tape, Repositionable Glue Tape* (apply by hand or with the Scotch *Glue Tape Dispenser 1093*), and *Photo & Document MOUNTING Tape*
- Specialty Tapes *Stitchery Tape* (specifically intended for mounting stitchery and delicate fabrics) and *Double-Sided Mounting Tape*
- Sunday International *Great Tape*
- Suze Weinberg *Wonder Tape*
- Therm O Web *Keep A Memory Acid-Free Mounting Adhesive Tape* and *Keep A Memory Acid Free Sticky Dots Adhesive Tape*
- Tombow *Permanent Mono Adhesive* and *Repositionable Mono Adhesive*
- TSI/Tape Systems *Transfer Tape* and *Heat Embossable Tape*
- USArtQuest *Ah, That's Great Tape*

Many of these tapes are offered in various widths.

Brands of double-sided, pre-cut mounting pieces include:
- 3L *Photo Fix*
- Fiskars *Photo Memories Photo Stickers*
- Pioneer *Photo Sticker Squares*
- Specialty Tapes *Master Tabs II*
- Therm O Web *Keep A Memory Acid Free Mounting Squares*

Photo Corners and Mounting Corners

Photo corners and mounting corners are self-adhesive on the back; items placed in these corners are not in contact with the adhesive and can be easily removed from the album or scrapbook. Photo corners are available in a variety of colors and clear. Mounting corners range in sizes from regular to jumbo; the larger sizes can be used for items such as certificates, documents, and posters.

Brands of self-adhesive photo corners include:
- 3L *PhotoCorners*, three sizes in Clear, White, Silver, Gold, and Black
- Fiskars *Photo Corners*, one size in Clear, Silver, Gold, and Black
- Pioneer *Photo Corners*, one size in Clear, Black, Metallic, and Rainbow (assorted colors)
- Therm O Web *Keep A Memory Acid-Free Photo Corners*

Project

Wedding Album Page

Designed by Pioneer Albums
©Pioneer Albums

You Will Need
Pioneer Albums 12- x 12-inch paper:
  White and black
Pioneer Albums *Colonial Cut Craft Scissors*
Pioneer Albums *Gold Photo Corners*
Pioneer Albums *Photo Glue Stick*
Pioneer Albums *3-D Self-Adhesive Gold Letters*
Pioneer Albums *Border Template*
1/16-inch hole punch
Photographs

1. Cut around the white paper with the *Colonial Cut Craft Scissors*. Punch a small hole in all of the points with the 1/16-inch hole punch. Using the *Photo Glue Stick*, bond the white paper to the black paper.

2. Cut black paper to mat the photographs with the same scissors and hole punch as in Step 1 so 1/4 inch is showing around photos.

3. Apply the photographs to the mats with the *Gold Photo Corners*. Using the *Photo Glue Stick*, bond the mats to the white paper in the desired position.

4. Draw an oval using the *Border Template*. Cut it out with the scissors and punch the edges.

5. Cut the paper chains by folding a piece of black paper along the length and carefully cutting (with the same scissors) along the fold so that just the edge of the pattern cuts into the paper. Unfold the cut paper; the small cuts on the fold become the center of the chain. Using the *Photo Glue Stick*, bond the chain to the corner of the page; bond the oval to the page.

6. Using the 3-D letters, place the names and dates on the oval.

Stickers and Adhesive Die-cuts

Stickers and adhesive die-cuts usually are not applied until after all photographs have been bonded to a page. Several are repositionable until burnished, allowing you the option of re-arranging them until the page design is to your satisfaction.

> There are dozens (and dozens) of brands of stickers and adhesive die-cuts. A few are:
> - Fiskars *Decorative Memories Stickers* and *Photo Memories Die-Cuts*
> - Frances Meyer, Inc. *Border Stickers, Frames, Letters,* and *Ransom Fun Stickers*
> - Paper Adventures *Create-Your-Own Stickers* and *Alphabets* (available in several colors)
> - Pioneer *Photo Caption Stickers* and *Self-Adhesive 3-D Gold Letters*
> - Provo *Alphabets, Alphabitties, Bitty Blocks, Border Stickers, Designer Stickers, Dress-Up Die-Cuts,* and *Sticky Die-Cuts*

Self-adhesive Embellishments

Self-adhesive embellishments described in Chapter 7 suitable for use in photo albums and scrapbook pages include: Delta *Renaissance Foil Instant Gilded Monograms,* Pamela Shoy Papers *Create a Border* and *Create a Quilt,* NuCentury *Fabulous Flower Pages* and *Fabulous Frames,* and Grafix *Funky Film* and *Really Funky Film.*

Repairing Photographs and Paper Items

You can repair torn and damaged photographs and paper items using Scotch *Photo and Document Mending Tape.* Place the item being repaired, back side up, on a non-stick surface. Adjoin the torn edges closely together. Place the tape over the tear and burnish to secure to the back of the item.

Self-adhesive Laminating Film

Self-adhesive laminating film protects items from finger marks, tears, and dust—a needed feature for items placed in photo albums and scrapbooks that receive heavy handling. UV-resistant laminating film is recommended for displayed items.

Read and follow the manufacturer's instructions when applying laminating film. If none are included on the package, apply the film to the front of the item, trim away excess, and burnish smooth from the center to the outer edges.

> Brands of self-adhesive laminating film include:
> - Grafix *Heavy-weight Laminating Film* and *Light-weight Laminating Film*
> - Therm O Web *Keep A Memory Acid-Free Self-Adhesive Laminate* in Matte and Gloss (smooth finishes), and *PeelnStick Acid-Free Decorating Laminating Sheets* in Linen and Leather (texture finishes)
> - Xyron cartridges

Spray Adhesives

Spray adhesives are either repositionable (temporary) or permanent. Regardless of type, apply only a thin layer of the adhesive; too thick an application may soak through the front of the item. Read and follow the manufacturer's instructions, and always spray in a well-ventilated room. The "spray box" described on page 56 eliminates a sticky work area.

Several spray adhesives can be removed from photographs with UnDu Products *un-du,* while some adhesives may require the use of either denatured alcohol or mineral spirits. Test on an unusable photo to be certain the product you have selected can be removed without damage to the photograph.

Repositionable spray adhesives must dry for a period of time after being applied; usually that time is less than 30 seconds. Often, these products also can be used for a permanent bond. In those cases, as it is with those labeled "permanent," the item is placed immediately on the surface to which it is being bonded.

Do not burnish items with a repositionable spray adhesive. Items with a permanent spray adhesive should be covered with either acid-free vellum or a reject photo (photo side down) and well burnished to secure the bond.

> **Brands of spray adhesives include:**
> - **3M *Spray Mount Spray Adhesive, Photo Mount Spray Adhesive,* and *Super 77 Adhesive***
> - **J. T. Trading Company *202* and *404***
> - **Sullivans *Make a Memory Ultra Adhesive Spray***

Hot Glues

Hot glues are generally acid-free, but read the label to determine if the hot glue you have selected is. Low-temperature glue sticks are recommended (brands of low-temperature glue sticks are listed on page 94). See Chapter 9 for more information on hot glues.

Place the item receiving hot glue face down on a non-stick surface. Apply the glue in a flat band along the item's outside edges. When bonding small dimensional items, place a dot of glue in the center back of the item. Position the item immediately; hot glues set very quickly. Do not burnish.

Use of hot glues on photographs and memorabilia is not recommended.

Solvent-based Adhesives

Solvent-based adhesives generally are not acid-free, although a limited number of products do qualify. Read the label to determine if the product you have selected is acid-free. Place the item receiving the adhesive face down on a disposal, non-stick surface (i.e. cooking parchment paper). Apply a thin band of the adhesive along the outside edges of the item. Position immediately, because these adhesive usually sets in a very short time. Do not burnish.

Use of solvent-based adhesives on photographs and memorabilia is not recommended.

Tips for Using Acid-free Adhesives

Handle photos and memorabilia as little as possible and only along the outer edges, and wear cotton gloves when working with fragile and delicate items. The oils and acids in your skin leave a residue that can have a deteriorating effect on these items over time.

As noted at the beginning of the chapter, save reject photographs. In addition to using them to protect photographs when burnishing, nothing is better for testing supplies. They also can be used to make stickers to embellish pages.

When cropping, save some of the scrap pieces. Use these scraps (and reject photographs) when testing adhesives and other supplies. If you use more than one film processing outlet, use a separate envelope for each; each may use slightly different photo paper.

Photo paper is glossy, and the back of a photograph is a semi-porous surface (some qualify as non-porous). The short time required for testing an adhesive—and any other supply used in an photo album or scrapbook—is your best guarantee that you will be satisfied with the results.

Paper punches turn cropping scraps and reject photographs into stickers that are color coordinated with the other photographs on the page. Place the reject into the punch with the photo side down. Place the punched designs, back up, on white tissue paper, and apply glue stick to the back of each. Pick up the designs with a tweezers and position them on the page. Cover each design with white tissue paper and burnish with your fingertip. If you prefer using a double-stick adhesive film or a *Xyron*, rather than a glue stick, place the adhesive on the back of the photograph (or cropping scrap) before punching. Punch with the release paper side up; remove the release paper and position the designs on the page. The McGills *StrongArm* makes punching the three layers (photograph, adhesive, and release paper) much easier. **Note:** It's best to stand when using larger-sized punches. In addition to cropping scraps and reject photographs, any acid-free paper (decorated or plain) can be used for making stickers following the same procedure.

Several crafting supplies are acid-free (be

sure to check the label) and suitable for embellishing pages in photo albums and scrapbooks. Products to consider include embossing powder, stamping inks, glitter (including Signature Crafts *Glitter Slivers*), Mylar die-cuts and spangles, and certain paints (Delta *Cherished Memories Acid-free Paper Paint* is formulated for use in photo albums and scrapbooks). **Note:** Due to the heat required for thermal embossing, do not place photographs on a page until after embossing is completed.

In addition to the correct adhesive, paper products included in photo albums and scrapbooks and for the storage of memorabilia must be selected with care. Look for those labeled archival, lignin-free, and/or acid-free. Lignin only applies to papers, not adhesives. A Fiskars *pH Testing Pen* provides an easy method to test the acidity level of the paper products you have selected.

Some paper products are not colorfast. To determine if a paper is colorfast, rub a dampened cotton swab across it. If the swab picks up color, it's best to use a double-stick adhesive film or tape for bonding, rather than a liquid adhesive.

If you possess the only remaining photograph of your great-grandparents for example, either have a photocopy made or scan the photograph. Use the photocopy or scan in the photo album or scrapbook; store the original photograph in a photo-safe, archival storage box. Archival storage boxes are available from Pioneer Album and University Products in a variety of sizes. Photocopies and scans allow for rule breaking: they're the solution when a project will receive heavy use and handling, or when supplies are not acid-free. **Note:** The intensity of the light required by some photocopying machines and scanners can cause damage to older and fragile photographs and documents. Most photography shops have a photocopier having a diffused light source specifically intended to safely copy photographs or documents. If you have questions concerning the use of a photocopier or scanner (with a photograph or document), consult a photography shop.

Album and scrapbook page protectors do exactly that: they protect pages from tears, finger marks, dust, and fading. All adhesives and supplies must be completely dry before placing a page in a protector.

Technique

Paperweight

Every proper Victorian home had at least one paperweight with a photograph on the back. A modified version of that type of paperweight can be made using either a photocopy or a scan, an acrylic block generally used for a rubber stamp, adhesive film, and self-adhesive laminating film.

Prairie Stamper offers acrylic blocks in three thicknesses in a large variety of sizes. The crystal clear blocks are beautifully finished with rounded corners, making them perfect for this project. In addition to use as paperweights (and blocks for stamps), they also are suitable for the display of copied photographs.

> **You Will Need**
> Photocopy of photograph that will be cropped to block size
> 3/4-inch thick acrylic block in needed size
> Craft stick
> Acid-free double-sided adhesive film
> Self-adhesive laminating film
> Miscellaneous supplies: plastic cook wrap, white tissue paper, scrap piece of vellum or cooking parchment paper, burnishing tool

1. Allowing for cropping, position the photocopy face up on the block. Use the side of a craft stick to gently push the sides of the photocopy over the sides of the block to form scored lines. Remove the photocopy from the block and cut along the scored lines.

2. Remove the release paper from one side of the adhesive film and place it over the front of the photocopy. Place a piece of plastic cook wrap over the back of the photocopy, covering the exposed adhesive film. The plastic wrap will prevent your scissors from sticking to the adhesive film when cutting and will fall away as you cut. With the covered adhesive side up, cut the film to the size of the photocopy. Do not remove the liner from the back of the film at this time.

3. Remove the release paper from the laminating film. Place the film on the back of the photocopy. Place a piece of plastic cook wrap over the front of the photocopy, covering all exposed adhesive on the laminating film. Cut the laminating film to the size of the photocopy.

4. Wipe off the back of the block with the wadded tissue paper. Remove the liner from the adhesive film covering the front of the photocopy. Position the photocopy on the back of the block. Cover with vellum or cooking parchment paper and burnish in place.

Note: Do not clean the block with either alcohol or window cleaner. Cleaning agents of this type have an adverse affect on acrylic surfaces.

Memorabilia

Experts disagree upon including memorabilia in either an album or a scrapbook with photographs. Some feel these items present the possibility of a negative effect upon photographs over time, and they recommend placing memorabilia in a separate album. All experts agree that memorabilia should be encapsulated, whether placed in the same album or scrapbook with photographs or in a separate one. Placing memorabilia in some type of enclosure also guarantees protection from damage that could result from handling. 3L *Memorabilia Pockets,* self-adhesive, envelope-like enclosures, are available in several sizes, and Therm O Web *Keep A Memory Acid-Free/PVC Free Memorabilia Pockets*, self-adhesive, envelope-like enclosures are available in three sizes. The raised compartments of a Plaid *Keepsake Keeper* displays dimensional objects in an album or scrapbook; an acid-free mat is included.

Memorabilia displayed on shelves, walls, and tables should be protected by UV-resistant materials and placed out of direct sunlight.

In addition to archival storage boxes, the University Products catalog (refer to Resources) offers a variety of UV-resistant materials. This catalog is an excellent source of valuable information regarding the care and preservation of photos and memorabilia.

Framed memorabilia, especially those of fabric, should be protected from contact with the glass and also the frame's backing. Frame Tek *Framespace, Rabbetspace,* and *Econspace* provide that protection. The spacers are easily and quickly applied; special tools are not required.

Photo albums, scrapbooks, and memorabilia should be kept in a stable environment. Excessive humidity can affect the bond of water-reversible adhesives and also have an adverse affect upon photographs and memorabilia. High temperatures and direct sunlight also can harm these items, in addition to affecting the long-term performance of many adhesives.

Project

"Home Tweet Home" Album Page

Designed by Colleen Rundgren for American Traditional Stencils
©American Traditional Stencils

You Will Need

American Traditional Stencils: *BL-914 Birdhouse* and *BL-911 Sunflower and Fence*

Shiva *Oilstiks*: Azo Yellow, Yellow Ochre, Sap Green, Alizarin Crimson, Burnt Umber, Prussian Blue, Black*

3/8-inch American Traditional Stencil Brushes, one for each color*

Beacon *Mounting Memories Keepsake Glue*

12- x 12-inch memory album page

Two sheets acid-free scrapbook paper: Blue

One sheet Paper Adventures: Green Gingham Check

One sheet Geopaper by Geographics Cloud Paper

One sheet 8-1/2- x 11-inch white Cranson Acid-Free Card Stock and scraps of various other colors

Two strips acid-free mat board, each 1/4 inch wide x 3 inches long

Fiskars *Paper Edgers*

Permanent acid-free fine tip black marker

Pencil and scissors

Optional: American Traditional Stencils *Light Table* and *Embossing Tool*

Photographs

*Available from American Traditional Stencils

1. Use the *Oilstiks* and stencil *BL-911* Sunflowers and Fence on the white card stock. Cut out, leaving a white border around the edges. With the pencil, trace Birds and Birdhouses from *BL-914* onto various colored card stock (i.e. brown for trees, etc.) and cut out. Treat each section separately so that the design is made from various colored papers.

2. With the *Mounting Memories Keepsake Glue*, bond the sheets of blue paper together to the album page, aligning them to left side of the page. Cut the Green Gingham Check paper into 1/4-inch wide strips; bond one strip along the right side of the album page. Bond the other four strips to the back of the Cloud Paper along the edges. Center the Cloud Paper onto the blue background of the album page and bond in place.

3. Bond the cutout Fence and Flowers along the bottom of the page. Cut small pieces from the end of the mat board strip made in Step 1. Bond the pieces to the back of the Flowers, then bond to the page to create a 3-D effect (see Step 5). Piece together and bond the Birdhouse, Tree, and Bird shapes to the page above the Flowers.

4. Using the *Mounting Memories Keepsake Glue*, bond small photographs to the Birdhouse shapes.

5. To make the fence sign, use the *Paper Edgers* to cut two 2-inch x 2-1/2-inch rectangles from different colored card stock. Bond the rectangles together, offsetting them slightly. Bond a small piece of the mat board strip to the back of the rectangles, then bond to the Fence to create a 3-D effect. Write a caption with the marker.

Chapter 9

Heat-activated Adhesives

Heat-activated adhesives include hot melt glues, embossing powders, iron-on fusible films and webs, and liquid fusibles. Depending on the adhesive, heat is supplied by a hot glue gun, glue kettle, heat gun, or iron.

Hot Glue Guns and Hot Melt Glues

Hot glue guns and hot melt glues were originally marketed to the construction trades and packaging industries. The first glue guns were unwieldy. Many did not have a trigger; the glue stick was pushed through the barrel with your finger. Glues were formulated for construction and industrial uses and were not suitable for several crafting materials. Even with those problems, the speed and convenience provided by the guns and glues did not go unnoticed by crafters; manufacturers responded by providing guns and glues specifically designed for crafting.

Composed of polymer and resin, hot glues are non-toxic; however, due to the heat required to melt these glues, they should not be used by young children, and older children should be closely supervised by an adult when using hot glues.

As seen here, guns are found in a variety of sizes, designs, and colors. Some offer the option of being used either corded or cordless (for example the Adhesive Technologies *Insty-Bond Tool* is completely cordless). Insulated nozzles reduce the possibility of burns, interchangeable nozzles apply glue in fine lines to wide bands, spring-tension nozzles prevent glue dripping from them unless the trigger is engaged, and triggers squeezed with your palm, rather than your index finger, reduce hand fatigue.

Regardless of the size, design, or color, all hot glue guns work on the same principle: An insulated heating chamber inside the gun heats the glue to the temperature necessary to melt it so it can flow from the nozzle.

Guns are available in mini, mid, and regular sizes in low, high, dual, and multi temperatures. Mini-sized guns are available in high and low temperatures (but not dual or multi temperatures) and feature a finger trigger and use a 4-inch long stick. Adhesives Technologies *Crafty Magic Melt Low Temp* guns use an oval-shaped stick;

other brands use round-shaped sticks. Models having insulated nozzles vary according to brand, and interchangeable nozzles cannot be used on a mini-sized gun. All mini models are corded. Mid- and full-sized guns offer a variety of features. In addition to low- and high-temperature models, several brands offer dual- or multi-temperature models.

With the exception of Adhesive

Technologies *Crafty Magic Melt Low Temp Bonder* and *Crafty Magic Melt Princess Mid-Size Trigger-Feed,* round sticks are used by all brands. The diameter required varies by model; depending on the type of glue, lengths range from 4 to 15 inches. Most guns mid- and full sizes can be used with interchangeable nozzles, several have insulated nozzles, and many offer the option of being used either corded or cordless. Triggers are either finger or palm squeezed. Some models have larger heating elements that melt the glue at a much faster rate than a conventional model.

Glue guns are sturdy tools and last a long time with minimal care. Before selecting a gun, consider the types of projects you will be doing and which features are best suited to those projects. The following models are only a portion of the guns offered by each brand.

Adhesive Technologies (Ad-Tech)
• *Cordless Insty-Bond Tool* is fueled by a small canister of butane (the type used for hair dryers) that provides up to one and a half hours of use; an on/off switch conserves fuel when not in use. The gun can be used with either high- or multi-temperature glues and is cordless.
• *Craft & FloralPro Glue Gun,* a low-temperature (290 degrees F) gun with a palm trigger, is packaged in a storage case containing four interchangeable nozzles, a wench, and an assortment of four specialty glues.
• *Professional I,* a regular-sized gun, has a spring tension nozzle and is packaged with five pounds of 10-inch industrial-strength glue and two interchangeable nozzles.

Bostik
• *HI-LO Dual Temperature Glue Gun* has an insulated nozzle, selection switch, and can be used with interchangeable nozzles.

Darice
• *Industrial Model Glue Gun,* a high-temperature gun, is designed for heavy use and can be used with interchangeable nozzles.

FPC/Surebonder
• *Double Heater Guns* are available in low- and high-temperature models. These guns melt glue twice as fast as full-size guns.
• *Dual Temperature Glue Gun Kit,* a corded model, is packaged in a storage case that includes six sticks of *All Temperature Glue* and two interchangeable nozzles.
• *Palm-Trigger Glue Guns* are available in low-, high-, and dual-temperature models in both mid and regular sizes. All models can be used with interchangeable nozzles.

H. B. Fuller
• *Dual-Temperature Hot Glue Gun* is a mid-size gun with an insulated nozzle.

Uniplast/Tecnocraft
• *ONEder Glue Gun* uses either low- or high-temperature mini sticks. Independent cartridges with a nozzle are placed in the Heating Station until needed. The cartridges quickly plug into the handle and eliminate purging when switching from one glue color or type to another. The gun can be used either corded or cordless.
• *Professional 3-Temperature Glue Gun* has three temperature settings (375, 400, and 425 degrees F) that are selected by a small knob. The nozzle is insulated.

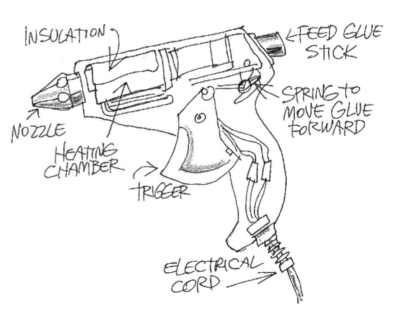

Flowered Frame, designed by Adhesives Technologies. The addition of silk flowers and foliage to a framed mirror provides the perfect decorating touch when display space is limited (like an entrance hall or half bath). Crafty Magic Low-Temp Floral Glue quickly bonds flowers and foliage to mirrors and other home decor items.

To extend the life of your gun, read and follow the manufacturer's instructions. Here are some additional suggestions:

• Allow the gun to reach operating temperature before depressing the trigger; larger guns may take up to 10 minutes to achieve that temperature.

• Do not place the gun on its side after plugging it into the outlet or turning it on; the nozzle should be pointed down when a heated gun is not being used. When finished working, allow the gun to cool in this position. After cooling, the gun can be stored in any position; the unused portion of the stick can remain in the gun (glue sticks have an indefinite shelf life).

• Don't pull or tug an unused portion of a stick from the gun; it must be purged from the gun.

• When finished working, unplug a gun and allow it to cool before using a cleaner to remove glue from the nozzle and gun. FPC/Surebonder *Glue Gun Cleaner* not only removes hot glue from guns, it also removes other adhesives, including stickers, from surfaces.

Purging

Purging is done by allowing the gun to reach operating temperature and squeezing the trigger until the stick is completely dispensed from the gun. Place a stick of clear glue (cut longer sticks to a 4-inch length) in the barrel behind colored or glitter glue to clean the barrel of color or glitter residue.

Purged glue does not have to go to waste. Either purge directly into a glue kettle or onto a non-stick surface (those specifically intended for hot glues are seen on page 11). Glue purged onto a non-stick surface can be peeled off the surface when cool and either be remelted in a kettle or softened with a heat gun.

While still warm, softened glue can be covered with another non-stick surface and rolled flat with a round object (bottle, piece of PVC pipe, etc.). Cooled glue that has set can be covered with a non-stick surface and pressed flat with a warm iron. Flattened glue can be cut into shapes and designs with scissors, rotary cutters, or a craft knife.

When a project requires several colors or types of glue, one option that saves purging time is to use several mini-sized guns, each having the color or type of glue being used. A multiple-outlet is a handy power supply when using several guns at one time. When working, place the heated guns on a non-stick surface (see photo on page 11). Any glue that drips from the nozzles can be peeled off the sheet when cool and used in the methods described on page 97.

The Uniplast/Tecnocraft *ONEder Gun* described earlier does not require the use of a multiple-outlet; the heating station requires only one plug.

Hot Glue Sticks

Hot glue sticks are either oval or round and are labeled as low-, high-, dual-, or multi-temperature. Hot glue sets as it cools. Although cure time varies according to the type of glue, most are at 50 percent of strength after one minute, 75 percent after one hour, and 100 percent after one day.

Adhesive Technologies *Crafty Magic Melt Oval* sticks are used only in *Crafty Magic Low Temp Guns*, while all other brands use round sticks. Mini-sized guns use either a 1/4- or 5/16-inch diameter stick; mid- and regular-sized guns (including Adhesive Technologies models) use either a 7/16- or 1/2-inch diameter stick. Color and glitter sticks are available only in a 4-inch length; other types range in length from 4 to 15 inches.

Low-temperature glues are formulated for surfaces that would be damaged by high temperatures, including man-made fabrics, *STYROFOAM*, balloons, certain plastics, fresh flowers, etc. Depending on type, these glues set from within 29 seconds to 3 minutes.

High-temperature glues form a strong bond and are intended for surfaces that are not damaged by higher temperatures. Depending on type, these glues set from within 30 to 90 seconds.

Dual- and multi-temperature glues are formulated for use in that type of gun; select the appropriate temperature required by the surfaces with the temperature switch. Although these glues also can be used in single-temperature guns (low and high), test to ensure satisfactory results.

Avoid using low-temperature glue in a high-temperature gun and vice versa. In both cases, the viscosity of the glue will be affected, and bonding may not be satisfactory.

Select the right glue for the project. Multi and all-purpose sticks are suitable for many surfaces; most labels indicate those best used. For jewelry, fabric, wood, floral, and polymer clay projects, select a glue formulated for those uses. With the exception of Adhesive Technologies' *Crafty Magic Melt Oval* sticks, other brands of hot glue sticks can be used in any brand of gun.

It's a temptation to buy unbranded sticks sold in bins, especially when they go on sale. These sticks are fine to use when purging a previous color stick from a gun or making embellishments, but they are not recommended for bonding. Inexpensive glue sticks may contain wax or other fillers that could greatly affect results.

Types of hot glue sticks by brand include:

- **Adhesive Technologies:** *Crafty Magic Melt Low-Temp Oval in Floral, Fabric, Jewelry, and Wood, Crafty Magic Melt High-Temp Round Glues in Crystal Clear, No Strings, Jewelry and Wood, Colorfun* (all purpose)
- **Bostik:** *0120* (for wood), *0130* (all-purpose with long open time), and *0140* (all-purpose with medium open time)
- **Darice:** *High Temperature Crystal Clear, Jewelry, Wood, Dual Temp, and Craft Designer* (all-purpose) in 5/16- and 7/16-inch diameters and *Low Temperature Colors and Glitters* in 5/16-inch diameter
- **FPC/Surebonder:** *Temporary Hold* in 7/16-inch diameter, *All-Temperature Glue, High Strength, High Temperature, and Amber Color* in 5/16-inch and 7/16-inch diameters, *Dual Temperature Fabric Stik, Jewelry Stik, Wood Stik, Best Stik and Polymer Clay Stik* in 5/16-inch diameters
- **Technocrat:** *Gloobies Hi&Lo* (dries clear), *High Performance* (dries dark tan), *Heavy Duty Clear, Glitter Hi&Lo, Glo-In-The-Dark Hi&Lo, Designer Color Hi&Lo, Neon Colors, Neon Colors Hi&Lo, Color Hi&Lo* (Globbies are available in both 5/16- and 7/16-inch diameters)

Donna Thomason has written several design books for use with colored Tecnocraft Globbies. The full-size designs are quickly and easily duplicated when covered with a Tecnocraft Glue Gun Pad shown here. Projects range in size from small animals to jewelry to larger projects. The examples shown are from her book, *Computer Pals*. The gun shown is the Uniplast/Tecnocraft *ONEder* Gun.

Hot Glue Tips

• All surfaces must be clean, dry, and free of dust and oil. Sanded surfaces must be wiped clean. If a surface is unaffected by rubbing alcohol, wipe it off with alcohol and allow to dry. Fabric projects (either yardage or purchased items) that will be laundered must be washed, dried, and pressed; do not use a softener in either the wash or dry cycles.

• Your fingers and hands should be dry when you're working. Hand lotion applied just prior to beginning can affect bonding.

• Have all supplies and tools ready before beginning. Hot glues set rapidly as they cool.

• Surfaces being bonded should be at room temperature. Non-porous surfaces often bond better if heated slightly with a hair dryer or heat gun before applying the glue; metal should feel very warm to the touch. Warmed surfaces also slightly extend the open time—the amount of time before the glue sets—allowing for more time to position items.

• Position the surfaces together quickly after applying the glue; usually only light pressure is sufficient to secure the bond.

• Work carefully to avoid burns. Glue gun manufacturers recommend having a bowl of ice water on your worktable while working. If you should accidentally touch either the nozzle or glue, immediately stick your fingers or hand into the water; do not attempt to remove the glue until it has cooled.

• Several crafters cut off the fingertips from old cotton gloves and tape them on their index fingers. You could also wrap a band aide over the tip of your index finger to protect it from burns.

• Use a section of paper towel folded four layers thick to wipe off the nozzle as you're working.

• Hot glue "stringies" are kept to a minimum when the opening of the nozzle is free of glue. Should strings form, lightly touch the nozzle to the glue and twist your wrist upward when lifting the gun away from the surface.

• Strings that form can be ignored as you're working. When finished, a slight touch with a hot nozzle will melt them away. A short blast (make it very short) from a heat gun or hair dryer also works.

Adhesive Technologies *No String Glue* is formulated to be string-free. A multi-purpose high-temperature glue, it can be used on several surfaces.

• When gluing very fragile surfaces (i.e. balloons), place the glue on the surface being bonded to it rather than the fragile surface. Then place the fragile surface on the glue. This allows the glue to cool slightly and reduces the possibility of the fragile surface being harmed. If bonding two fragile surfaces together, spread the glue on a craft stick, quickly apply the glue to one of the surfaces, then position the surfaces together.

• When decorating glass ornaments with hot glue, hold the gun's nozzle slightly above the surface of the glass; do not allow the nozzle to come in contact with the glass. Wear gloves to avoid cuts should the glass break.

• When applying hot glue to fabric, apply it in a flat band to avoid glue "ridges" showing through the fabric. The band of glue should be between 1/8- and 1/4-inch wide; too narrow a band may not provide the necessary bonding.

• Fabric items with hot glue cannot be dry-cleaned. Follow the manufacturer's instructions when laundering; most do not recommend placing items in the dryer. If pressing is necessary, place a hot glue work pad (see page 11) on the board and another over the glued area.

• For projects that will be exposed to extended high or low temperatures, use care when selecting glues. Some glues withstand temperatures exceeding 100 degrees F, while others withstand below freezing temperatures; however, it's best not to place hot-glued items in direct sunlight if you live in a warm climate, or to leave them outdoors in the winter if you live in a cold climate.

• If the bond should weaken, often a heat gun or hair dryer will soften the glue so that the surfaces can be pressed together again. Use an iron at low heat to soften glue on fabric projects; place a non-stick surface over the glued area to avoid getting glue on the iron. Do not apply too much heat, because you only want to soften the glue until it is tacky (remember to test).

Project

Fan Pin

Origami paper brushed with Polyform *Liquid Sculpey* is durable and suitable for jewelry. Non-metallic papers are the best choice for this technique. To make matching earrings, use a smaller square of the paper and attach earring backs.

You Will Need

4-inch square Yasutomo *Origami Paper*

8-inch piece Yasutomo *Mizuhiki Cord*: Gold

Polyform *Liquid Sculpey*

Small bristle brush

Pin back with plastic plate on top of pin

Clover Needlecraft, Inc. *Straight Tailor's Awl*

Round toothpick

Hot glue gun

FPC/Surebonder *Polymer Clay Hot Glue* stick

1. Make a fan from the origami paper by fan folding the 4-inch square. Tightly squeeze the folds at the lower end of the fan. Going from side to side of the squeezed end, punch a small hole with the awl.

2. Place the toothpick in the punched hole. Brush a light coat of *Liquid Sculpey* over the back of the fan. Cure, following the directions on the *Liquid Sculpey* package. When cool, brush a light coat of *Liquid Sculpey* over the folded edges on the front of the fan. Cure according to the label instructions. When cool, remove the toothpick.

3. Cut the piece of *Mizuhiki Cord* in half. Thread both pieces through the punched hole at the base of the fan. There will be two pieces of cord on either side of the punched hole; all four pieces should be the same length. Using all four pieces, tie a knot on the front of the fan base. Twist the cords tightly to form a tail on each side of the fan base.

4. Insert the glue stick into the gun; allow to heat. Apply a thin band of glue along the plastic plate on the top of the pin. Immediately position the pin to the back of the fan. Allow to cool.

These pins were also assembled with the help of hot glue.

Creative Options

Hot glues offer a variety of creative options. Although they are considered primarily for bonding, don't limit these versatile glues to that use only.

Hot glue sticks can be cut into small pieces and placed under a surface, creating height for a dimensional effect. Cut pieces from a stick in the needed size (with scissors or a craft knife). Lightly touch the nozzle of gun to one end of the cut piece and place that end on the back of the item being elevated; press to secure the piece to the surface. Lightly touch the nozzle on the other end of the cut piece and position it on the background surface; press to secure. When longer pieces are needed, cut the stick in the length needed to fit across the back of an item. Lightly run the nozzle down the entire length of the stick and position it on the back of the item; press to secure. Lightly run the nozzle along the other side of the stick and position it on the background surface; press to secure.

Another method is to form dots of glue on a non-stick surface. Extrude the amount of glue in the width and height needed. When cool, remove the dots from the non-stick surface. Either touch the nozzle to the front and back of the dot as explained above, or place a small dot of glue on the front and back of the dot to secure it between the two surfaces.

Most glue sticks are acid-free (check the label) and can be used for scrapbooks and with memorabilia (see Chapter 8).

Glue extruded from the gun can be rolled flat between two non-stick surfaces. Place a puddle of glue on a non-stick surface and cover with another non-stick surface. Immediately roll with a round shape (rolling pin, piece of PVC pipe, glass, etc.) to flatten the glue. Flatten pieces can be used as the base for jewelry, cut into shapes using scissors, decorative edgers, rotary cutters, or a craft knife, rolled into designs, or used to create dimension.

Glue directly from a glue gun can be dispersed into candy, soap, cookie, and polymer clay molds to create pins and surface embellishments. To avoid the glue from sticking in the mold, thoroughly coat the inside of the mold with a liquid the glue will not adhere to, like glycerin (purchase at drug store), embossing ink, pigment ink, or mineral oil. Use a small brush to apply the liquid into the mold. If the liquid should puddle in the mold, remove the excess with a dry brush or cotton swab. **Note:** Sculpey *Flexible Push Molds* are made from a non-stick material and do not required being coated prior to use with hot glue.) After filling the mold with glue, it can be placed in the freezer to hasten cooling. When cool, the glue is easily removed from the mold. The flex provided by both fabric and polymer clay glues make them a good selection for this technique. Molded glue shapes can be painted with acrylic paint, rubbed with Craf-T *Rub Ons* or powdered pigments (Magicalfaerieland *Faerie Dust*, Jacquard Products *Pearl Ex*, Lemon Tree *Powdered Pearls*, and Twinrocker *Pearlescent Powdered Pigments*). Applying an acrylic varnish to the finished piece is optional.

Glue Kettles or Skillets

Glue kettles or skillets are used for melting glue sticks, pre-cut pieces of glue, and purged glue that has set. The pre-cut pieces are often referred to as hot melt, bundles, chips, or pellets; glue sticks also can be cut into small pieces.

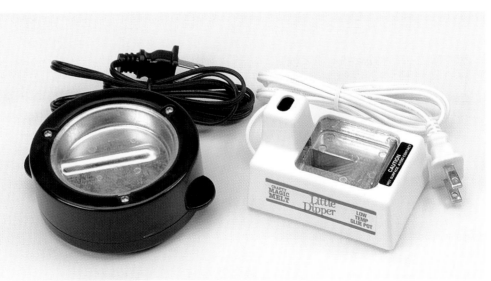

To keep clean-up to a minimum, spray the inside and outside of the pot with a *Silicone* spray; allow to dry before plugging in the kettle. Spraying will be necessary each time the kettle is used. To change colors or types of glue in the kettle, plug in the kettle and allow the glue to melt. Dump the hot, melted glue onto a non-stick hot glue work surface (refer to hot glue gun accessories in the next column). Wipe out the kettle with paper towels folded four layers thick. Use caution, because the kettle and glue will be hot.

A kettle is especially handy when applying glue to the tip or base of small items and when spreading glue over the surface of small items. Use tweezers when dipping small items, particularly flower stems, into the glue. You'll find the long-handled tweezers on page 13 are much easier to use than cosmetic tweezers.

One word of caution when using a kettle or skillet. Repeated heating of hot glue, either pre-cut pieces or sticks you cut, will carbonize the glue, making it unstable. To avoid unsatisfactory results when using a kettle or skillet, use a fresh batch of glue each time. Don't add more glue than you think you will use at one time; throw away what remains when you are finished working. Do not reheat glue purged from a gun more than once.

Use a sturdy, disposal, flat-edged item (like a charge card, craft stick, or piece of mat board) to spread glue. A "handle" made from a reusable adhesive (refer to page 59) placed on the underside of the item keeps your fingers glue- (and burn-) free when spreading the glue. The handle also provides a cooling platform; just stick it to a flat surface.

Brands of kettles include:
- **Adhesive Technologies** *Crafty Magic Melt Little Dipper*
- **Darice** *Glue Pot* (4-inch diameter)
- **FPC/Surebonder** *Kettle* (4- and 7-inch diameters)
- **Suze Weinberg** *Hot Pot* (4-inch diameter). In addition to having an on/off switch, the *Hot Pot* is Teflon-lined and can be used for melting hot glue and thick embossing powders.

Brands of pre-cut pieces include:
- Bostik *Hot Melt MY1505*, which sets quickly, and *Hot Melt MY-4205* has a medium set time
- Darice *Glue Bundles* are all-purpose
- FPC/Surebonder *Diamond-Cubes* are non-stringing
- Tecnocraft *Hot Glue Chips/Pillows Hi&Lo* dries clear, and *Chips/Pillows High Performance* dries dark tan

---

Hot Glue Gun Accessories

Hot glue gun accessories include those from Adhesive Technologies, Darice, FPC/Surebonder, Suze Weinberg, Tecnocraft, and Tower Hobbies.

Adhesive Technologies and FPC Surebonder interchangeable nozzles are available in a variety of sizes and fit most brands of mid- and regular-sized guns.

The Holster Deluxe by Tecnocraft holds either a mini- or regular-sized gun, plus sticks and other supplies; a non-stick tile protects surfaces from dripping glue.

Non-stick, translucent, work surfaces include:
- **Adhesive Technologies** *Craft Work Surface* in 8- x 8-inch, 12- x 12-inch, and 18- x 18-inch sizes
- **Darice** *Glue Gun Pad* in 8- x 8-inch size
- **FPC/Surebonder** *Glue Gun Pads* in 8- x 8-inch and 19- x 19-inch sizes
- **Tecnocraft** *Glue Gun Pads* in 5- x 7-inch and 7- x 7-inch sizes

---

Due to the heat-resistant and non-stick features of these surfaces, they are excellent work surfaces for many crafting activities. When dry, most supplies (with the exception of glues intended for bonding plastic) are quickly and easily removed. Should any linger, securely press strips of Manco *Duck Tape* over them and lift the tape.

Heat Guns

Heat guns are yet another crafting tool that began life in building supply stores. These guns can reach very high heats, with some models heating to 1100 degrees F. Use caution when using a gun reaching heat of that level. One other word of caution: Although these guns closely resemble a hair dryer, they should **never** be used for that purpose.

Uses for heat guns include: to soften or melt hot glues, heat certain types of fusibles, dry paint and liquid glue, set fabric paint and markers, heat puff fabric and craft paints, melt embossing powder, heat all brands of shrink plastics, soften *Friendly Plastic*, heat craft foam, and heat Clearsnap, Inc. *MagicStamp*.

Brands of heat guns include:
- **Darice (single-heat)**
- **Surebonder (single- and dual-heat)**
- **Suze Weinberg (single-heat)**
- **Tecnocraft (single-heat)**
- **Tower Hobbies (dual-heat)**

Craft Foil

Place craft foil, shiny side up, on warm, softened glue. Rub the foil gently to secure it to the glue; remove the clear covering from the foil after the glue has cooled. Place metal leaf on warm, softened glue and cover it with a piece of the paper inserted between the sheets of leaf in the book (the term used for the leaf's packaging). Lightly rub on the paper to adhere the leaf to the glue; as much as possible, do not touch the leaf with your fingers. Remove the paper after the glue has cooled. Use a soft brush to remove any leaf that is not bonded to the glue. Apply a finish to the leaf to keep it from tarnishing.

Enhancements can be placed on warm glue, covered with a non-stick surface then rolled. Enhancements to consider include small glass beads, powdered pigments, Craf-T *Rub-Ons*, trims, shrink plastic designs, punched or cut shapes of ColArt Americas *Glass and Tile Colors Specialty Metal Sheets*, and small charms. Remove the non-stick surface covering the glue and heat the glue slightly (very slightly) with the heat gun to secure the bond.

A rubber or polymer stamp, or other shaped item (buttons, charms, cookie cutters, etc), can be pressed into softened glue. The surface of the stamp or item must be well coated with embossing ink, pigment ink, or glycerin before being pressed into the glue. Allow the glue to completely cool (a trip into a freezer quickly hastens the cooling) before removing the stamp or item. Powdered mica pigments, Craf-t *Rub-Ons*, or acrylic paint can be rubbed over the surface to highlight the pressed design.

A small amount of hot glue applied either to the surface receiving an embellished design or to the back of the embellishment will secure them together.

To secure items to thumb tacks and push pins, cover a kitchen sponge with freezer paper. Push tacks or pins into the sponge through the freezer paper. Apply a small amount of glue to the top of the tack or pin and immediately place the item on the glue. Press lightly to secure. When cool, lift the tack or pin from the sponge. Any glue that oozed from under the design will not stick to the freezer paper.

Examples of embellished tacks and push pins: The polymer clay faces (1) were purchased, a quilt block stamp, ©Pelle's See-Thru Stamps from Purrfections (2), was stamped in black Fimo polymer clay that had been mixed with silver metal leaf, black Lucky Squirrel PolyShrink was stamped with a sponge stamp and thermal embossed with white embossing powder (3), and both roses were molded in the American Art Clay Co. Fimo Roses Mold (4) (one was hot glue that had been rubbed with Faerie Dust, the other from the tacky glue/cinnamon "recipe"; refer to Chapter 3.

Shrink Plastic

All brands of shrink plastic can be heated for shrinking with a heat gun. The gun should move back and forth when heating; hold the gun approximately 4 inches above the plastic. The plastic will twist, turn, and jump around during the heating process. Using the tip of a wooden skewer to hold the plastic down controls some of the action. If heated in a 4-inch deep cardboard box, there's less chance of the plastic taking flight across the room. Heat the plastic until it is flat. If it is not flat after shrinking, cover the warm plastic with a piece of wood and apply pressure.

Depending on the brand, the plastic will shrink from 33 to 60 percent of the original size. Punch holes needed for wire embellishing (or other type of dingle-dangle accessories) prior to heating. If rounded corners are desired on the finished piece, do this before heating with a corner punch, decorative edge scissors, or plain scissors. Coloring can be done either before or after heating. If done before heating, the colors will be intensified. Stamp prints must be made with a permanent ink (Clearsnap, Inc. *Ancient Page* or *Crafter's Ink*, for example). Some brands recommend light sanding the plastic before heating; follow the manufacturer's instructions.

In addition to all-purpose hot glue (mentioned on page 91), several glues and adhesives can be used for bonding the plastic to pin backs or other pieces of plastic. These products also bond embellishments to the plastic.

Lucky Squirrel *Ultra Thin Bond*, a heat-activated adhesive film, is specifically designed for use with all brands of shrink plastic; a heat gun is needed for heating the film. Permanent pressure sensitive adhesive films and tapes (refer to Chapter 7) are suitable, as are most of the solvent-based adhesives described in Chapter 10; however, use discretion when selecting one of these adhesives—an epoxy is hardly needed for shrink plastic.

Friendly Plastic

American Art Clay Co., Inc. *Friendly Plastic* softens very quickly with a heat gun; do not overheat. Hold the gun's nozzle a least 6 inches above the plastic and move the gun back and forth across the plastic at all times. To make larger pieces, butt the edges of two warmed pieces together and reheat slightly. Place a hot glue non-stick work surface over the plastic and smooth the junction flat (the Scratch-Art *Rubbing Stick* works wells for this).

Softened *Friendly Plastic* can be impressed with rubber stamps that have been inked as directed for stamping in hot glues. Allow the *Friendly Plastic* to completely cool before removing the stamp. Both craft foil and metal leaf can be placed on the plastic while it is still warm. Embossing powder can be sprinkled over the plastic after it has become warm; continue heating until the powder melts.

Pressure sensitive adhesive film or tape suitable for thermal embossing (refer to Chapter 7) can be placed on the back of the plastic before heating. The release paper should be left on the exposed side until the plastic has cooled. Remove the release paper to bond the plastic to another surface.

Other suitable adhesives for *Friendly Plastic* include all-purpose hot glue and most of the solvent-based adhesives (refer to Chapter 11). As mentioned for shrink plastic, use discretion when selecting a solvent-based adhesive.

Thermal Embossing

Thermal embossing with embossing powders is quickly done with a heat gun. Other sources of heat can be used, including a light bulb, warming plate, toaster, or oven but frankly, they're a hassle to use! Ultra detail, fine, regular, and thick embossing powders are used with stamped prints. After being embossed, the the stamped print will have a shiny, raised appearance, similar to that of thermographic printing seen in commercial printing. With few exceptions, embossing powder is acid-free.

Embossing powders are affected by humidity and must be stored in airtight containers away from heat and direct sunlight. Placing a piece of macaroni or a small silica packet (found in vitamin bottles and shoe boxes) in the container helps control moisture absorption by the powder. Think Ink recommends using its metallic *Liquid Glass* within six months from date of purchase.

All embossing and pigment inks (Clearsnap, Inc. *ColorBox Ink*, *Crafter's Ink*, and *Top Boss Embossing Ink*, Stewart Superior, Corp. *Imprintz*, etc.) dry slowly and allow time to apply embossing powder over the ink (the powder sticks to these inks). Stamps inked with pads having these inks produce prints that can be thermal embossed; pads also can be patted over a surface when more complete coverage is desired.

Genesis *Artist Colors* are an oil-based, semi-solid paint that is suitable for use with embossing powder and apply easily to a stamp with a foam dauber (Darice *Embossing Essentials* are available in two sizes). Either a brush or rubber brayer can be used to apply the paint to larger surfaces. If not thermal embossed, the paint requires heat setting to dry. Read the manufacturer's instructions prior to use.

After stamping prints or applying the ink or paint over the surface, cover the inked area with the embossing powder. Place a piece of scrap paper (vellum is a good choice because the powder doesn't stick to it) on the work surface. Turn the item over and tap sharply on the back; powder that did not stick to the ink will fall off on the paper. Turn on the gun and wait a moment for the gun to reach operating temperature.

Place the item with the embossing powder on a flat, heat-resistant surface (hot glue work surfaces are excellent). Holding the gun 4 to 6 inches above the embossing powder, aim the nozzle at one area until the powder begins to melt and the color changes. Do not move the gun back and forth, because that only delays the time required for the powder to get hot enough. As the powder in an area is melted, aim the nozzle at an adjacent area. Continue in this way until all powder is melted. Return the powder on the scrap paper to the jar.

Another method of applying embossing powders to a surface when complete coverage is desired is to spray the surface with a repositionable adhesive (refer to Chapter 6). Allow the adhesive to become tacky before applying the embossing powder. Tap off the excess powder and heat as directed above.

Think Ink *Foil & Flock*, an adhesive embossing powder, becomes tacky when briefly heated with a heat gun. Do not overheat; heat **only** until the powder changes color. *Foil & Flock* bonds craft foil, metal leaf, and lightweight embellishing supplies (see suggested supplies for softened hot glue on page 97) to porous surfaces.

Thick embossing powder is often referred to as enamel. The granules of this type of powder are much larger and usually are not suitable for highly detailed stamped prints. It is most commonly used when complete coverage of a surface is desired, for bonding items, and being impressed with a stamp or other formed item.

Thick embossing powders are adhesive when at least three layers are applied to a surface. After the first layer of powder is melted, more powder is immediately applied to the still hot layer. Excess powder is tapped off on scrap paper (vellum is recommended because the powder doesn't stick to it) and the remaining powder is melted. These steps are continued until the desired thickness is reached. When used as an adhesive, items must be placed in the hot, melted powder immediately; embossing powder cools and sets very quickly.

Colors of powder can be combined during this process, creating new colors and accents. To control "fly-away" of the powder as it's heated, place the item in a cardboard box that is larger than the item and at least 4 inches deep.

If you find melting multiple layers of thick embossing powder somewhat frustrating, consider either *Foil & Flock* or a repositionable spray adhesive. Regardless of which method you select, tap off the excess powder prior to heating a layer.

Foil & Flock instantly becomes tacky when sprinkled over a layer of the heated embossing powder, so no additional heat is required. The next layer of embossing powder sticks securely to the powder. When using a spray repositionable adhesive, allow the melted powder to cool for about 20 seconds before spraying. When the adhesive is dry (it still will be tacky) cover with another layer of powder.

Suze Weinberg has created several techniques using *UTEE* melted in the *Hot Pot* offered by her company. Items can be dipped into the hot *UTEE* for coating, or the melted powder is allowed to cool and removed from the pot. The resulting pieces can be used to create embellishments.

Pieces of melted embossing powder must be bonded to a stable, firm surface to keep them from breaking and cracking. Permanent pressure sensitive adhesive films and tapes (refer to Chapter 7) are the easiest and fastest supplies to use for bonding. Therm O Web *Make A Memory Acid-Free Sticky Dots Adhesives* do not require cutting away excess adhesive extending beyond the edges of the piece and are an easy PSA to use on irregular-shaped items.

Clearsnap, Inc., Judi-Kins, Ranger Industries, Inc., Stewart Superior, and Think Ink offer a wide range of colors and types of embossing powders in ultra fine, detail, and regular-sized granules.

Brands of thick embossing powder include:
- Judi-Kins *Amazing Glaze*
- Stewart Superior *Imprintz Embossing Enamel*
- Suze Weinberg *Ultra Thick Embossing Enamel (UTEE)*
- Think Ink *Liquid Glass*

Iron-on Fusibles

Iron-on fusibles in web and film forms are available in yardage, pre-cut pieces, and tapes. Previously, these adhesives were used only on fabric and applied with an iron, but today, fusibles are used on all porous surfaces; some also can be used on non-porous surfaces. An iron is still the primary heating source, although some techniques and products are better suited to a heat gun.

Tips and Techniques

Surfaces must be dry and dust- and oil-free before applying a fusible. Surfaces not affected by rubbing alcohol should be wiped off with it and dry before beginning. It is very impor-tant that the manufacturer's directions are read and followed when using a fusible on fabric (yardage or purchased items) that will be laundered.

In almost every case, a fusible is first applied to the wrong side of one surface. That surface is placed, right side up, on another surface. Heat is generally required for both steps.

Fusibles that require steam when used for fabric can be used with most papers without steam; a heat suitable for the paper usually will be sufficient. Cover fragile paper with a *Teflon* pressing sheet (see photo on page 11) to avoid damaging or scorching the paper. Test to ensure satisfactory results.

Before using a fusible, protect the ironing board or work surface by covering it with cooking parchment paper, a *Teflon* pressing sheet, or by pressing freezer paper to the cover.

If the fusible you have selected does not have a release paper on at least one side, cover it with either a *Teflon* pressing sheet or cooking parchment paper before beginning the first step.

When fusing, do not slide the iron from place to place; the iron should be lifted as the position is changed. Position the iron so that steam vents are not over the outer edges of surfaces being fused; areas under steam vents often do not bond well. The Clover Needlecraft, Inc. *Craft Iron* (see page 15) does not have steam vents and is an excellent iron to use for fusing (in addition to other crafting techniques).

Do not disturb fused surfaces until cool. Moving the item prior to cooling often affects the bonding properties of a fusible.

When using a heat gun, use the tip of a wooden skewer to hold the surfaces in place when applying heat.

When a fusible "Oops!" happens (and it will), place a double thickness of white tissue paper over the area and press with a hot iron. Immediately pick up the tissue paper. Refold it following each pressing and repeat as needed until all fusible is lifted from the surface. Another method is to cover the errant fusible with Manco *Duck Tape*, rub briskly to secure the tape firmly on the fusible, and lift the tape. Repeat as needed.

Fusibles generally easily wipe off irons with a *Teflon*-coated sole plate (the bottom of the iron), and Dritz *Iron-Off Hot Iron Cleaner* removes fusibles from irons without a *Teflon*-coated sole.

Dry cleaning will remove fusible residue when a fused appliqué has been removed from fabric.

Rather than cutting out shapes or appliqués before applying the fusible, apply the fusible to the wrong side of the entire piece of paper or fabric being used for shapes or appliqués, then cut out. When cutting out shapes or appliqués, rotate the surface you are cutting, not the scissors. The scissors tips should be pointed directly in front of you when cutting. Grade the edge by slightly angling your cutting hand over the surface being cut. This will leave a tiny edge of fusible beyond the edge of the cut shape and will bond the edges more securely. Remove the release paper from the fusible, position the shape or appliqué on the surface, and press.

Paper punches can be used on paper after a fusible has been applied to it. Position the paper in the slot with the paper side up. Use the tip of a wooden skewer to hold punched shapes in place when fusing to another surface.

Apply a fusible to the back of lightweight papers to use as torn paper pieces in collage and other layered techniques. Arrange the pieces in the desired design and press in place on a background surface (card stock, mat board, foam core, wood, etc.) **Note:** Aleene's *Stick N Hold* and Lucky Squire *Ultra Thin Bond* cannot be used for this technique.

To fuse fabric lace and trim (and paper laces and doilies) to surfaces, apply the fusible to the wrong side of the lace or trim. Gently pull away any fusible that extends beyond the lace or trim edges. Place, right side up, on the surface to which you are bonding. Cover the lace or trim with a double thickness of white tissue paper. Press, using the tip of the iron around open areas. Immediately pick up the tissue paper. Any bits of tissue paper that linger on the fabric can be removed with a damp cotton swab.

Slightly heat metal with a heat gun or hair dryer before placing the fusible on it. Cover metal with a brown grocery bag to protect the iron when pressing.

Cindy Walter's book, *More Snippet Sensations* (refer to Inspirations) includes instructions for fused quilts and framed fabric art projects. After applying a fusible to the wrong side of fabric, the fabric is cut into pieces necessary for the desired design. The same technique can be used with paper (either cut or torn pieces), resulting in fused decoupage.

To create a double-sided appliqué of either fabric to paper, fuse the wrong sides together. After the appliqué has been cut out, it be can be bonded to a surface with fusible tape, liquid fusible, fabric glue, white glue, acrylic-based adhesive, or pressure sensitive adhesive tape. Double-sided appliqués can be used in pop-up cards and for dimensional fabric appliqués.

It is important to follow the manufacturer's directions regarding the heat of the iron and the use of steam for fabric projects (either yardage or purchased items) that will be laundered.

Before beginning, wash and dry all fabrics being used; do not use a softener in either the wash or dry cycles. Press to remove all wrinkles.

Muslin and denim fabrics may require several washings to remove all sizing. Test by sprinkling a few drops of water on the fabric; if the drops are quickly absorbed, the sizing has been removed.

Perma-press fabrics and fabrics treated with soil, fire, or water repellants often do not provide satisfactory results; test before using these types of fabrics.

Read the label to ensure the fusible you have selected is the type needed. Some require either stitching or applying dimensional fabric paint around the outer edges of appliqués to keep them in place, while some should not be stitched.

Project

Quickie Banners

Designed by Mary Mulari, Mary's Productions

You have to agree these banners look a bit classier than the "marker on cardboard" variety. A plus: stitching is not required when making these washable banners. This technique also can be used for making decorative flags to use on special days.

Instructions for making a casing used for the doweling, the button thumbtacks (another of Mary's ideas), and adding the ribbon flower follow.

You Will Need

Fabric that is 1-1/4 inches longer and 1-1/4 inches wider than the finished size of the banner

Assorted fabrics for the lettering and design*

Therm O Web *HeatnBond Ultra-Hold 5/8-inch Pre-Measured Width*

Therm O Web *HeatnBond Ultra-Hold Iron-on Adhesive*

Scissors, pinking shears, iron, ironing board, pencil, tracing paper

Optional: 1/4-inch doweling slightly longer than the banner, cording (approximately 12 inches long); three thumb tacks, three buttons, Eclectic *E-6000*, kitchen sponge, small piece of freezer paper; ribbon flower, narrow ribbon

Mary Mulari's Book, Appliques with Style *(refer to Inspirations) has a variety of alphabets and designs suitable for tracing.*

To Make the Banner: Following the manufacturer's directions for iron temperature and pressing time, fuse the 5/8-inch wide *Ultra-Hold* to the each edge along the wrong side of the fabric. Closely trim each fused edge with a pinking shears (if you do not have

pinking shears, use scissors). Remove the release paper, turn the fused edges to the wrong side of the fabric, and fuse in place. Allow to cool.

To Add Letters and/or Designs: Trace the needed letters and/or designs; if larger letters or designs are desired, enlarge the tracings on a photocopier. Cut out along the traced lines. Place the tracings right side down on the paper covering the back of *Ultra-Hold Iron-on Adhesive.* (**Note:** In Mary's book, all letters and designs are in reverse and are placed right side up on the paper). Trace the letters and/or designs on the paper. Cut along the traced lines. Position the letters and/or designs on the front of the banner. Fuse in place. Allow to cool.

To Make a Casing for a Dowel: Cut a piece of fabric that is approximately 2 inches shorter than the top of the banner and 2-1/2 inches wide. Press a 1/4-inch hem along both 2-1/2-inch sides to the wrong side of the fabric. Fuse 5/8-inch wide *UltraHold* on the wrong side of the fabric to one long edge of the fabric. Remove the release paper and fold the fabric in half so that the pressed hems are on the inside. Fuse the long edges together. Fuse 5/8-inch wide *UltraHold* along the top of this fused edge on the right side of the fabric. Remove the release paper. Position this strip of fabric on the wrong side of the banner so that the edge with the fusible is below the top of the banner; fuse in place. Allow to cool. Slide the doweling into the casing and tie the cording to each end of the doweling to use as a hanger.

To Make Button Thumbtacks: Apply a thin layer of *E-6000* to the top of a tack. Immediately position a button on the tack, pressing it firmly in place with your fingertip.

Repeat for the other tacks. Allow the glue to cure before using the tacks.

To Add the Ribbon Flower: Tie a long bow in the narrow ribbon. Place a dime-sized drop (a larger flower will require more) of *E-6000* on the banner where the flower is desired. Immediately place the ribbon bow on the glue and cover with the ribbon flower. Press firmly in place with your fingertip. Allow the glue to cure before handling the banner.

Unless otherwise noted, the following brands of fusibles in film and web forms are suitable for all porous surfaces and are heated with an iron, while those suitable for non-porous surfaces and those suitable for use with a heat gun are indicated. Follow the instructions provided on each product's label or packaging.

Dritz
• *Stitcher Witchery* (available in yardage, pre-cut pieces, and tape)

Freudenberg Nonwovens/Pellon Division
• *Wonder Under*

Lucky Squirrel
• *Ultra Thin Bond* (for non-porous surfaces only; use of a heat gun recommended; not suitable for stitching)

Therm O Web
• *Iron-On Curtain Repair Tape* (not suitable for stitching)
• *Iron-On Make-A-Patch Fabric Repair Adhesive* (not suitable for stitching)
• *Iron-On Rug Repair Tape* (not suitable for stitching)
• *Iron-On Upholstery Repair Tape* (not suitable for stitching)

• *Iron-On Upholstery Repair Patch* (not suitable for stitching)
• *Iron-On Window Shade Repair Patch* (not suitable for stitching)
• *HeatnBond Ultra Hold Iron-On Adhesive* (available in yardage, pre-cut pieces, and tape, including *Quilter's Edge*; suitable for most non-porous surfaces, test; not suitable for stitching)
• *HeatnBond Lite Iron-On Adhesive* (available in yardage, pre-cut pieces, and tape, including *Quilter's Edge*)

Warm Company
• *Steam-A-Seam* (available in yardage, pre-cut pieces, and tape; suitable for non-porous surfaces)
• *Steam-A-Seam 2* (available in yardage, pre-cut pieces, and tape; light adhesive on each side of the fusible allows for repositioning of items before pressing; the bond is permanent when pressed)
• *Beads-2-Fuse* (suitable for non-porous surfaces)

What's New, Ltd
• *Fus-O-Bond* (suitable for non-porous surfaces; suitable for use with a heat gun)

Project

Fancy Jeans

Embellished clothing is back in style, and jeans are at the top of the list. Applying embellishments to plain jeans not only provides a custom look, but it's also a great money-saver.

You Will Need

Jeans
Trims of your choice*
Warm Company *Steam-A-Seam 2*: 1/2-inch wide tape
Iron** and ironing board
Scissors, white tissue paper, cotton swab

* Saint Louis Trimming *Appliqué Art* (trim and appliqués) was used in the example.
**Set iron at temperature recommended by the manufacturer listed on tape's package.

---

1. Wash and press jeans. Measure around one bottom cuff; double the measurement and add 1/2 inch to that measurement. Cut a piece of trim in that length and cut that piece in half. Each piece of trim will be the measurement of a bottom cuff, plus 1/4 inch.
2. Place *Steam A Seam 2* on the wrong side of the trim, along the upper edge. Finger-press in place.
3. Remove the release paper. Butt one end of the trim next to the inner leg seam of one cuff; the lower edge of the trim should not extend beyond the bottom of the cuff. Finger-press the trim in place along the cuff of that leg. Fold the second end of the trim back 1/8 inch; cover the folded area with a small (less than 1/4 inch long) piece of *Steam A Seam 2*. This piece should not extend beyond the end of the trim. Place the folded end over the leg seam and the unfolded end of the trim.

Adjust the length of the trim if necessary. When adjustments are complete, finger-press the trim in place again. Fuse the trim to the cuff. Use the tip of the iron to securely fuse the folded end of the trim.
4. Repeat for the second leg.
5. Place the appliqués, wrong side up, on a flat surface. Cut pieces of tape in the length needed to cover the appliqués; place them, with the sides touching, on the back of the appliqués. Finger-press the pieces of tape in place. Remove the release paper and gently pull away any fusible extending beyond the edges of the appliqués.
6. Position the appliqués on the jeans (the example shows one at the top of the pocket, and the other on a leg). Finger-press in place.

7. Cover the appliqués with a double-thickness of tissue paper. Fuse to the jeans; immediately pick up the tissue paper. If any fusible is still visible along the outer edges of the appliqués, use a new piece of tissue paper to cover them and use the tip of the iron to press those areas. Any tissue paper remaining on the jeans can be removed with a wet cotton swab.

Products With Fusibles

Products with a fusible in place are time-savers and serve many uses. Read and follow the manufacturer's instructions; the method of application varies for each of the following products.

Cache Junction *Fabric Fiber Iron-Ons* can be fused to almost every surface, including glass. These colorful appliqués withstand heavy use (and repeated laundry) without fading. *Soft Touch Velvet Iron-Ons* have the look and feel of velvet, yet can be washed and dried in the machine. Another feature: both products are acid-free and can be used in scrapbooks.

Clover Needlecraft *Quick Bias*, a pre-folded, fusible bias tape, can be used on all porous surfaces. Available in a wide range of colors, including metallics, this tape is especially effective for Celtic designs and stained glass appliqué. Designs are quickly duplicated when covered with a Clover Needlecraft *Quick Bias Design Sheet*, a translucent, pinnable, non-stick surface; the tape is formed in the shape of the design on the *Design Sheet* and pressed in place on the sheet. When cool, the design lifts easily from the non-stick surface of the sheet and is ready to be fused to a porous surface. Crafters, especially stampers, find this tape a valuable addition to their supply stash. Because it is a bias, circular and folded designs are easily made. The tape also is used for pin weaving, another popular technique used for embellishing porous surfaces; pin weaving designs can be formed on the *Design Sheet* in the same manner followed for Celtic or stained glass design. The fusible on *Quick Bias* is not permanent; stitching is required when used on fabric that will be laundered.

Dritz *Mending Tape* is available in a variety of colors and fabrics, in both tape and pre-cut pieces. It's an excellent patching fabric and also an excellent fabric for stamping.

Stamped designs colored with fabric markers (two brands are Dylon and Zig) can be cut out and used either as fused patches or fused decorative appliqués on porous surfaces. The heat required to fuse *Mending Tape* to a surface will set the fabric markers, making them permanent. *Mending Tape* does not require stitching when used on fabric that will be laundered.

Dritz *Iron-On Letters and Numbers* make quick work of adding names to clothing, especially T-shirts and sweatshirts. Other suggestions include notebook covers, backpacks, banners, and storage boxes.

HTC *Craft Plus*, a soft, low-loft, non-woven material, is particularly handy when multiple layers of a low-loft material are desired for covering boxes and picture frames, and when making place mats and wall hangings. When pressed together, layers of *Craft Plus* do not shift during construction.

Fabric and paper can be placed on the fusible layer and pressed in place; the fusible layer can be placed on wood and pressed in place. Usually, one layer of *Craft Plus* is sufficient for a slightly padded appearance. Lisa Shepard includes projects using *Craft Plus* in her book, *African Accents* (refer to Inspirations).

June Tailor *Quilter's Fusible Batting* has a thin fusible on each side. When placed between the top and back of a quilt and pressed, it is not necessary to either baste or pin the quilt before tying or quilting. The fusible can be removed from the quilt by laundering in cold water.

Sulky *Iron-On Stabilizers* are often thought of only as a stitching supply; however, they offer several options for other crafting activities. The non-woven material is not affected by liquids; it will not wrinkle or shrink. These two features make them an excellent choice for a type of paste paper (refer to Really, Really Faux Paste Paper on page 48). When dry, the "paper" can be fused to another surface. Sulky *Iron-On Stabilizers* are available in black and white in various weights. These stabilizers quickly fuse to porous surfaces, including mat board, card stock, and wood. The soft hand of the stabilizers makes them an easy supply to use when a mitered corner is desired and when covering round shapes. After being fused to a surface, the stabilizers can be embellished with paint, stamp prints, glass beads, craft foil, metal leaf, plastic jewels, charms—just about anything. To embellish with embossing powder, spray the stabilizer with Sulky KK2000, allow to become tacky, cover with embossing powder, shake off the excess powder, and heat.

Therm O Web *Iron-On Vinyl* is a laminating supply suitable for a wide range of surfaces due to the low heat required for fusing. A low tack adhesive on the back of the vinyl holds it in place for positioning and when pressing. What's New Ltd. *Cabin Fever Fabric Appliques* kits include die-cut designs with a fusible in place.

Freezer Paper

Although it's somewhat of a stretch to consider freezer paper a fusible, it is an excellent supply to fuse to tissue paper. The resulting paper is strong, opaque, and folds and creases well enough to be used for origami.

Press the tissue paper with a medium-heat iron until it is smooth and flat. Place the freezer paper, shiny side up, on the ironing board. Cover with a piece of tissue paper that is slightly larger than the freezer paper. Using a low-heat iron, press the tissue to the freezer paper. Increase the heat to medium; press again to secure the bond. If necessary, use the tip of the iron to smooth any wrinkles in the tissue paper. Allow to cool.

Tissue/freezer paper is suitable for use with decorative scissors and paper punches. It can be thermal or pressure embossed. In addition to origami folding, it can be used for torn collage, and layered pieces, self-made envelopes, gift

bags, and gift wrap. If desired, the freezer paper layer can be decorated with stamp prints or acrylic paint when used for envelopes and gift bags.

When cutting with decorative scissors, or using a paper punch, cut or punch with the freezer paper side up. Bond cut and punched shapes to surfaces with paste, white glue (PVA), a glue stick, or a pressure sensitive adhesive. Refer to Chapter 7 for an easy method to remove release paper from pressure sensitive adhesives when used with punched designs.

Because pressure embossing can be done on either the tissue or freezer paper side, consider using both positive and negative pressure-embossed designs in a piece.

Brands of pressure-embossing supplies include:
- **American Traditional Stencils in *Brass* and *Aluminum***
- **Darice *Embossing Essentials Brass Stencils***
- **Fiskars *Paper Crimper***
- **McGill *EmbossArt***
- **Paper Adventures *Lil' Boss* and *Big Boss***

All Green Sneakers templates, *Kreate-a-lope, Kreate-a-bag, Bagamites, Kreate-a-pop,* and *Kreate-a-box,* can be used with tissue/freezer paper. The templates also can be used with other supplies that have been fused using an iron-on fusible. Consider paper-to-paper, paper-to-fabric, and fabric-to-fabric. An envelope or gift bag with a lamè lining is quite special.

The envelope shown on the next page was made with the Green Sneakers *Kreate-a-lope* template using Bemiss-Jason Antique Gold *Luster Tissue* that had been fused to freezer paper. The template was placed on the freezer paper side, and the tissue/freezer paper was torn around the edges of the template. No cutting is required when this template is used.

The leaf seal was made using Polyform *Liquid Sculpey* that had been spread in a thin layer over the copper leaf form and sprinkled with various colors of regular embossing powders. The heat of the oven required to cure *Liquid Sculpey* also melted the embossing powders. After cooling, the leaf easily lifted from the copper form. Therm O Web *Keep A Memory Acid-Free Sticky Dots Adhesive* bonded the leaf to the flap of the envelope. **Note:** Although *Liquid Sculpey* seals made in this way are very thin, extra postage may be required; check with the post office before mailing.

What's New Ltd. *Artic Applique Pre-cut Freezer Paper Shapes* are used for creating fabric appliqués. The shapes are removed after the appliqué is stitched to the background fabric.

Liquid Fusibles

Liquid fusibles are generally used on fabric, although they can be used on papers. When used with fabric (yardage and purchased items) that will be laundered, the heat and pressure provided by an iron are necessary for this type of fusible; use of a heat gun is not recommended.

Apply to fabric as directed on the label;

place a *Teflon* pressing sheet on the ironing board and over the fabric when pressing. Before beginning, fabric should be prepared in the same manner as described in Tips and Techniques for iron-on fusibles.

When applying trims and lace to fabric, apply the fusible to the wrong side of the trim or lace. When dry, position these items on the fabric; press in place.

Although liquid fusibles bond paper layers without heat, the bond will be stronger if pressed. When pressing, place a *Teflon* pressing sheet on the ironing board and over the paper. If not pressed, the paper layers should be joined together immediately; do not allow the fusible to dry.

Brands of liquid fusibles include:
• Aleene's *Liquid Fusible Web*
• Beacon *Liqui-Fuse*
Follow the laundry instructions on the label; both products can be dry cleaned.

109

Chapter 10

Warnings Are Included

The labels on the adhesive products included in this chapter contain warnings, ranging from a single line stating that the product should not be used by young children, to specific directions for the correct use of the product and mentions of possible health risks.

Carefully read and follow all manufacturers' safety instructions. Always have the opening of the container pointed away from you as it is opened; some labels recommend the use of safety glasses when using the product. Do not eat, drink, or smoke when working with products mentioned in this chapter. Proper ventilation is very important; open doors and windows to ensure adequate air flow. Several are highly flammable and cannot be used in close proximity to open flame. Wash your hands immediately when finished working.

It's very important to properly store these products; they should remain in the original container, tightly closed, out of direct sunlight, and out of the reach of children. Some require following guidelines for disposal.

As stated in Chapter 1, if you have any questions concerning the correct use of a product, or possible heath problems that could result from use of a product, contact the manufacturer and request the MSDS (Material Safety Data Sheet). In almost every case, manufacturers of solvent-based products include their phone number on the product label. Many manufacturers of solvent-based products with a website include the MSDS for those products on the site; the Acknowledgments in the front of this book includes the URL for companies having a site at press time.

Aerosols

The warnings found on a can of spray adhesive are primarily due to the propellant. In addition to being highly flammable, the odor and fumes of most propellants require proper ventilation.

Spray adhesives apply quickly and dry almost instantly. They are found in three types: permanent, repositionable, and dual-use. Those that are permanent are applied to one or both surfaces which are joined together immediately. Those that are repositionable are applied to one surface and allowed to dry until tacky; the two surfaces are then joined together. Dual-use products can be used either for a permanent or temporary bond, depending upon the method of application. When the surfaces are joined together immediately, the bond is permanent; when the adhesive is allowed to dry until tacky, the bond is temporary. The label will indicate the type of bond provided by the product you have selected.

Mineral spirits and solvent-based cleaners remove spray adhesives that go astray, and rubbing alcohol can be used if the amount of adhesive is very light. It's much easier not having to worry about clean-up by using a spray box (see page 56).

As with all adhesives, apply only the needed amount. Two light applications are better than one heavy application. For larger surfaces, apply the spray in a horizontal direction, then in a vertical direction to ensure all areas are coated with the spray. Unless directed to the contrary on the container, burnish the top surface when a permanent bond is desired.

Before use, thoroughly shake the can. Make

sure the nozzle opening is pointed away from you; usually there will be an arrow or some type of marker indicating the opening. If the adhesive does not come out in a fine spray, the nozzle may be clogged. Turn the can upside down and depress the button until only air is escaping. Shake the can and begin spraying again. If the nozzle is still clogged, remove the button and clean out the opening with a small pin (**do not** put the pin into the opening at the top of the can!). If it is still clogged, soaking the nozzle in rubbing alcohol overnight often removes the remaining glue.

Pin Beaded Pin Cushion, designed by Victoria Waller. The technique of using straight pins and small glass beads to create a beaded design on a padded surface dates back to Victorian times. Thanks to spray adhesives, making the padded surface is much easier and faster today. Also helpful are Dritz Pins for Pin Beading, which are intended specifically for this craft. More of Victoria's designs can be seen in Design Originals Pin Beading Book.

When spraying a large area, it may be necessary to stop spraying and shake the can now and then. As soon as the adhesive begins to spit and splat, stop spraying and shake the can.

When finished, turn the can upside down and depress the button until only air is escaping (do this in the spray box). Replace the cap on the can. Store in a cool place, out of direct sunlight.

Spray adhesives can be used on almost every surface. They are an easy adhesive to use when bonding, paper and fabric lace, and trims having open areas to a surface.

A repositionable glue sprayed to the back of stencils eliminates the need for taping them in place. In addition to the products mentioned here, other repositionable spray adhesives suitable for the back of a stencil are described in Chapter 6.

Certain types of plastic foam can be affected by the propellant. Test before beginning.

The nozzles of 3M *Hi-Strength 90* and Bostik *Super Tak* have an adjustable spray setting. This feature is especially handy when applying a spray adhesive to either small or confined areas. Other spray adhesives include: 3M *Photo Mount* and *Super 77*, Bostik *Foam & Fabric*, Delta *Stencil Magic Spray Adhesive*, FPC/Surebonder *355*, Krylon *All-Purpose Spray Adhesive*, and Plaid *Priscilla Hauser Stencil Adhesive*.

Additional spray adhesives are described on page 54.

Cements

Depending upon the product, cements form a medium to strong bond; viscosities range from medium to very thin. All are water-resistant, set in a reasonably short amount of time, and are suitable for several surfaces. Flex is generally limited.

With few exceptions, cements can be used with wood, glass, ceramics, porcelain, metal, leather, rubber, and paper. Most are suitable for hard plastics, and many are suitable for fabric; however, several are not suitable for use on hard plastic foam. Refer to the label of the product you have selected to determine if it is suitable for the surfaces being used in your project. Surfaces should be clean, dry, and free of oil and grease.

If the label does not mention a recommended solvent for removal of the adhesive, use either acetone, a non-oily, acetone nail polish remover, or mineral spirits. Dry cleaning removes some, but not all, of these adhesives from fabric.

Some manufacturers recommend using their product as a contact cement (the adhesive is applied to both surfaces). Apply the adhesive in this manner only if it recommended by the manufacturer. UHU *Glu Contact Cement* is not a liquid; it is packaged in a twist-up tube, similar to a glue stick and is easily applied to the surface.

Germanow-Simon Corp. *G-S Cement* is packaged in a tube with a very fine applicator tip that allows for precision placement of the cement. The small white bottles shown on page 11 are *G-S Precision Applicator Refillable Bottles*. The bottles can be filled with any liquid that will flow through the tip when precision application is desired.

Other features worth noting: National Artcraft Co. *Glass Hold* bonds crushed glass and other hard grainy supplies (small glass beads, etc.) to non-porous surfaces, Scotch Super *Strength All Purpose Adhesive* is dishwasher safe (top rack), and UHU *Model & Hobby Glue* is impervious to model fuels. Other cement products include: Bond *527 Multi Purpose Cement* and *Victory 1991*, and National Artcraft Co. *All Hold*.

Project

Money Makes the World Go 'Round

Every trip to a foreign land produces a pocket-full of change that didn't get spent. Rather than leaving those vacation reminders in a drawer, place them on a frame holding a picture from the trip to continue the memories.

You Will Need
Metal frame, in desired size
Assorted foreign coins
Photograph*
Bond *527 Multi Purpose Cement*
Miscellaneous supplies: Small disposable pan, craft stick, vinegar, small cloth
*Photograph shown ©Susan Gillen

1. Remove the glass and easel back from the frame. Dilute the vinegar with an equal part of water. Wipe off the frame with the diluted vinegar; allow to dry.

2. Arrange the coins on the frame. Squirt a small amount of the adhesive on the disposable pan. Using the craft stick, apply the glue in a light coating to the back of a coin. Reposition the coin in place on the frame. Continue in this manner until all coins are bonded to the frame. Leave flat until dry.

3. Put the glass in the frame. Position the picture behind the glass. Replace the easel back.

High-tech Adhesives

Although the formulas of these product differ greatly, all form a flexible, strong bond, are gap-filling, and are suitable for a variety of surfaces. Some are water- and weather-proof. Depending upon the product, viscosity varies from medium to very thick.

Surfaces should be clean, dry, and free of oil and dust. Wipe off non-porous surfaces with rubbing alcohol or vinegar diluted with an equal part of water and allow to dry before applying the adhesive.

When used for bonding, apply only the needed amount. Thicker products are often used on the back of an item to create a dimensional effect in a project. In this case, apply the amount needed for height; allow the adhesive to cure before moving the project.

These adhesives set quickly, but cure time varies by product. In some cases, clamping bonded surfaces will be recommended by the manufacturer. Once dry, they are very difficult to remove. Most labels recommend using either lacquer thinner or xylene for removal. Dry cleaning removes a limited number of these products from clothing.

To eliminate the problems encountered when squeezing those of a thick viscosity from a tube, use either a tube gripper or a paper crimper. Use care not to get any adhesive on the crimper's rollers!

FPC/Surebonder *Cool Glue Gun* and Bond *Cool-Bonder Applicator* are often described as the alternate to a hot glue gun. Both brands use glue cartridges that are dispensed with a trigger mechanism, in much the same manner as a hot glue gun. The combination of the trigger mechanism and the small applicator tip on the cartridge allows you to easily and accurately extrude a fine bead of adhesive. Although the cartridges are similar in appearance, do not use the cartridge of one brand in another applicator.

The FPC/Surebonder *CG-9000* cartridge is a clear, all-purpose adhesive suitable for a variety of surfaces. Bond *CoolGlue* cartridges, in Regular and Jumbo sized cartridges, include: *Red Glitter, Gold Glitter, Blue Glitter, Cool Gloo* (clear, all purpose), and *Foam Glue* for hard plastic foams.

In addition to wood, Franklin International *Titebond Polyurethane Glue* is suitable for metal, ceramics, certain plastics, and cement. This adhesive is moisture-curing; if the humidity is extremely low, it may be necessary to wipe off the surface with a damp sponge before applying the adhesive. To ensure satisfactory results, read and follow the directions on the label.

Other brands of high-tech adhesives include:
- Aleene's *Platinum Bond Super Fabric Textile Adhesive, Platinum Bond 7800 Industrial Strength Craft Adhesive,* and *Platinum Bond Patio & Garden Outdoor Adhesive*
- Eclectic Products, Inc. *E-6000*
- FPC/Surebonder *9000 Adhesive & Sealant*
- Quick Grap, Inc. *Quick Grab*
- UHU *All Purpose Glue*

Project

Decorated Gift Box

Designed by Barbara C. Bosler,
B & B Etching Products, Inc.

Receiving a gift in a decorated box doubles the pleasure. The time required to make this exquisite box is surprisingly short, and your extra attention is guaranteed to be appreciated.

You Will Need
etchall *etching crème*
etchall *Happy Holidays pre-cut adhesive stencil*
etchall *squeegee*
Paper maché box (example box is 3 x 4 inches)
etchall Mirror (example is 2 x 3 inches)
Decorative trim to go around mirror
Flat braid to go around both the rim of lid and the base of box
Gold acrylic craft paint
One 3/4- x 2 3/4-inch piece of double-sided adhesive film
FPC/Surebonder *Cool Glue Gun* and *CG-9000 Cartridge*
Small brush

1. Using the gold paint, paint the inside of the box. When dry, paint the outside of the box. Allow to dry.

2. Follow the manufacturer's directions for the placement of the stencil on the mirror and application of the *etching crème* to etch the mirror. Allow to dry.

3. Apply the double-sided adhesive film to the back of the mirror. Remove the release paper from the adhesive film and center the mirror on the lid of the box. Press to secure the mirror to the lid.

4. Place the *CG-9000 Cartridge* in the *Cool Glue Gun* as directed by the manufacturer and apply a bead of glue around the edges of the mirror. Immediately position the trim on the glue. Press in place with your fingertips.

5. Using the *Cool Glue Gun*, apply a bead of glue around the rim of the lid. Immediately position the braid on the glue. Press in place with your fingertips. Apply the braid around the base of the box in the same manner. Allow the glue to cure before handling the box.

Epoxies

These are the muscle-men of the adhesive world. Not every product has the same bonding power, but an epoxy usually will provide a stronger bond than any other type of adhesive. Use an epoxy when that strength is needed, but not when the resulting bond will be stronger than the surfaces, like soft woods.

An epoxy is composed of two parts, a resin and a hardener. Those two parts must be mixed together before the epoxy can be applied to a surface. Epoxies are found in three forms: individual containers of resin and hardener which are mixed together in the ratio directed by the manufacturer, side-by-side barrels with a single plunger that releases the correct ratio of the resin and hardener for mixing together, and squeeze-type pouches that allow for mixing the resin and hardener within them. Loctite *Poxy Pouches* are a "squeeze, knead, open, and use" epoxy.

Surfaces should be clean, dry, and free of oil and dust. Wipe off non-porous surfaces with mineral spirits, acetone, or a non-oily acetone fingernail polish remover. Allow to dry.

When using an epoxy that requires mixing the resin and hardener, prepare the surfaces being bonded before mixing the epoxy. Using a craft stick or toothpick, mix the resin and hard-

ener in the ratio directed by the manufacturer on a disposable palette (piece of cooking foil, disposable cooking pan, etc.). UHU *Glu 5-Minute Epoxy Works!* dispenses the resin and hardener in the proper ratio on the mixing palette; no measuring is required. Mix only the needed amount, because mixed epoxy cannot be stored. Immediately apply mixed epoxy to the surfaces.

Apply epoxy carefully and only in the needed amount; remove excess immediately with mineral spirits, acetone, or a non-oily acetone polish remover. To remove epoxy that has set, soak the item overnight in Hughes Associates *Attack*, then clean the surfaces with acetone. *Attack* is methylene chloride, so use with extreme caution.

Set and cure times vary by product. Select a product that has a fast set for smaller projects; products with a slow set allow more positioning time and are easier to use for larger projects. The surfaces should be stable and secure during the set time. Clamps, clear tape, or masking tape can be used to hold surfaces in place. Do no use the item until cure has been reached (the label will tell you how long that period is). After curing, epoxy can be sanded, painted, and drilled. Most will withstand the temperature of a dishwasher.

Project

Found Treasure

It hardly seems possible this candleholder once held tuna fish. Artifacts *Metal Carvings* turn the can into a beautiful holder.

You Will Need

Empty tuna fish can
Artifacts *Metal Carving Leaves*
Loctite *Poxy Pouches*
Miscellaneous supplies: Rubbing alcohol, small cloth, craft stick, aluminum cooking foil for work surface, small clamps
Optional: Small piece of pressure sensitive felt for bottom of can

1. Wash and dry the interior and exterior of the can. Bend the leaves to conform to the curve of the can; determine the arrangement of the leaves on the can. Remove the leaves; set aside. Wipe off the outside of the can with rubbing alcohol; allow to dry.

2. Cover the work surface with aluminum foil. Following the manufacturer's instructions, blend one pouch of the epoxy.

3. Squirt a small amount of epoxy on the work surface. Using the craft stick, apply a light coating of epoxy to the back of one leaf section. Position in place and clamp. Repeat for the other leaf sections until the can is covered. Leave clamps in place for 24 hours.

4. If desired, apply a circle of felt to the bottom of the can (to protect tabletops).

Instant Glues (Cyanoacrylate)

As the name implies, these products form a bond almost immediately upon contact. Some have a short (very short!) open time, but no other type of adhesive bonds as quickly as an instant. Needless to say, having everything for your project ready is a requirement when working with an instant glue. Cure time varies by product and ranges up to 24 hours. Do not use the glued item until full cure has been reached.

Follow all manufacturers' instructions carefully; some recommend wearing safety glasses and plastic gloves when working. Point the tube away from your face when opening it. It's wise to have a tube of instant glue remover handy whenever you use one of these adhesives. Should your fingers get stuck to anything, use an instant glue remover to loosen them. Pulling them apart or from a surface can remove skin.

> **Brands of instant glue remover include:**
> - **Ross**
> - **Satelite City**
> - **SureHold**

Although suitable for a wide variety of surfaces, certain plastics, fabrics, and foam rubber are rarely recommended for use with instant glue. Generally, manufacturers recommend gels on non-porous and vertical surfaces and liquids on porous and close fitting surfaces. Use an accelerator (same brand as the glue) when a liquid is used with ill-fitting surfaces.

In almost every case, instant glue is applied by the drop—literally. Apply only the needed amount, because excessive amounts decrease the bonding ability of the glue. SureHold *Brush-On Super Glue* is intended for those times when a thin coating of glue would be better than a drop of glue.

Surfaces must be clean, dry, and free of dust and oil. Moisture is the bane of instant glues; all surfaces must be absolutely dry. In high humidity areas, dry the surfaces with a hair dryer at low heat. Allow to cool before applying the glue. If you've had problems with the bond of an instant glue not holding, humidity may have been a factor.

Unopened tubes can be stored in the refrigerator to extend the shelf life, but it's not recommended if there are children (or teenagers who will eat anything in the fridge!) in the home. Allow the glue to reach room temperature before use. Do not store opened tubes in the refrigerator, because moisture can render the glue useless. Once opened, the shelf life of the glue is approximately six months; a gel generally has a longer shelf life than a liquid. Replace the cap tightly to keep moisture from entering the tube.

After opening, don't use a pin as a stopper in the opening of the tube or bottle; you'll end up with a container of instant glue with a permanent pin-stopper. Fortunately, manufacturers are designing containers that close tightly after being opened. SureHold *"Drip-Proof, Clog-Proof" Super Glue* and UHU *Super Glue Pipette* are two products offering that feature.

For those who have difficulties in squeezing a small tube of instant glue, products packaged in small bottles include:

- Bostik 7434 (for porous surfaces) and 7432 (for rubber and plastic)
- Loctite *QuickTite Super Glue Gel* and *QuickTite Super Glue*
- Satelite City *Hot Stuff Special "T" Ultra Gap-Filling,* and *Hot Stuff Thick UFO*
- SureHold *Brush-On Super Glue*

In addition to those previously mentioned, other brands of instant glue include:

- FPC/Surebonder *Super Glue Thick Glue* and *Super Glue*
- Loctite *Instant Glass Glue* (dishwasher safe)
- Ross *Super Glue Gel* and *Super Glue Liquid*
- Scotch *Super Glue Gel*
- SureHold *Plastic Surgery Super Gel* (Don't be surprised by "surgery" for the SureHold product. Instant glue is often used in surgery, but the formula is altered for medical purposes.)

Silicone Adhesives and Sealants

Silicone adhesives are unaffected by moisture and weather and are suitable for almost every surface. They provide tremendous flex and are very durable. The thick viscosity makes them a good choice when the surfaces being bonded are not level and flush. The viscosity also prevents these products from seeping through thin, porous surfaces. If silicone adhesives have a disadvantage, it is their inability to accept paint or stain.

Surfaces should be clean, dry, and free of oil and dust. Wipe off non-porous surfaces with rubbing alcohol and allow to dry before applying the adhesive. Depending upon the brand, set time ranges from five to 20 minutes. Complete drying may take as long as 24 hours, while cure time may take an additional 24 hours.

Remove excess immediately from porous surfaces by scraping with a craft knife. When an excessive amount is on a hard finish, non-porous surface, allow the adhesive to dry then cut off the excess with a craft knife.

Although silicone is non-toxic, it can irritate eyes and skin prior to drying. Use only with adequate ventilation. When finished working, immediately wipe off your hands, all work surfaces, and tools with paper towels. Wash your hands with soap and water and clean work surfaces and tools.

In addition to being used to bond surfaces together, a silicone adhesive or sealant is an easy-to-use supply for creating dimension. Squirt a "dimple" of the adhesive on the background surface and cover with the item that is to be raised above the surface.

Chapter 11

Rx for Special Jobs

The adhesive products described in previous chapters are suitable for use on a variety of surfaces and for several techniques; however, there are certain products specifically designed for particular surfaces and techniques. These products often provide better results than those of a more general nature.

Stitchless Sewing

Fabric glues can be used with either yardage or purchased clothing. Whenever a fabric project will be laundered or dry cleaned, select a glue carefully. To avoid purchasing the wrong type of glue, look for laundering and/or dry cleaning directions on the label. Often, "washable" indicates that the glue is not permanent and is removed when laundered. Select the glue appropriate for the type of fabric being used. A cotton T-shirt requires a glue that can be laundered and will stretch with the fabric, while a velvet pillow requires a glue that can be dry cleaned. Thin viscosity glues usually are not recommended for sheer fabrics.

Water-based fabric glues tend to dry slowly. Prior to drying, most are easily removed from fabric by laundering. To completely remove dried glue, dry cleaning is usually the best solution. *KissOff Stain Remover* will remove some, but not all, dried water-based fabric glues.

Solvent-based glues generally dry rapidly; rubbing alcohol, acetone (non-oily nail polish remover can be substituted), mineral spirits, and dry cleaning remove dried glues. Test on an inconspicuous area to ensure the selected supply does not damage the fabric or remove color.

Treated fabrics (perma-press, stain resistant, fire retardant, water repellant, etc.) usually do not bond well. The solutions used for treating the fabric prevent glue (and paint) from penetrating the fibers. Some synthetic fabrics, especially those with a slick finish, also may not bond well.

Washable fabrics should be laundered, without a softener in either the washer or dryer, before applying glue, an iron-on fusible, hot glue, or paint. Muslin and denim usually have to go through several wash cycles to remove all sizing. Sprinkle a few drops of water on the dry fabric. If they are absorbed by the fabric, the sizing has been removed. Sizing left in fabric prevents the glue from forming a strong bond.

All fabrics, including those that are dry clean only, should be pressed smooth and flat before beginning.

Some type of barrier must be placed on the wrong side of the fabric before applying glue. Shirt and pants boards are available in most crafts stores in the fabric paint department. The fabric should be smooth and taunt on the board and secured with clips, long bobby pins, straight pins, or T-pins.

Another option is to press freezer paper to the wrong side of the fabric. In addition to being an excellent barrier, it holds the fabric smooth and taunt and prevents the fabric from wrinkling and bunching up as glue is applied. Place yardage on a flat work surface; a piece of cardboard can be placed inside a shirt or pant leg, or they can be placed on a flat surface.

When applying glue to a shirt sleeve, slide a plastic soda bottle (usually the 2-liter size works best) inside it. Push pins through the sleeve into the bottle to hold it securely to the bottle while applying glue. Allow to dry for 24 hours (longer if the humidity is high). During that time, do not remove the fabric from the board, work surface, or plastic bottle; if freezer paper was pressed to the wrong side of the fabric, leave it in place. To ensure that glue has fully cured, allow two weeks before laundering or dry cleaning.

Follow the manufacturer's directions when applying the glue. Some recommend applying glue only to the edges of an appliqué or trim, while others recommend covering the entire back surface of an appliqué or trim. Too much glue results in a big gooey mess, so apply only the needed amount.

It may be necessary to seal the surface of lightweight fabrics with a very light coating of glue before applying the amount needed for a secure bond. Allow the sealer coat of glue to dry before applying a second, slightly heavier, coat of glue.

When bonding either trims or appliqués to fabric, mask adjoining areas to keep them glue-free. Position the trim or appliqué on the surface to which it is being bonded. Place masking tape on the surface so that one edge of the tape is along, but not over the outer edges, of the appliqué or trim. Pick up the appliqué or trim. Following the manufacturer's directions, apply the glue to the back of the appliqué, trim, or the fabric. If applied to the fabric, apply within the area surrounded by the masking tape. Place the appliqué or trim on the fabric. Use either a Clover Needlecraft, Inc. *Finger Presser* or your fingertip to lightly tap the trim or appliqué in place and to secure the bond.

Heavier trims or appliqués usually require being weighted until the glue has dried. Cover the trim or appliqué with a *Teflon* pressing sheet or cooking parchment paper and place weight (books, Olfa *Sewing Weights*, etc.) on the pressing sheet or parchment paper. The weight should be evenly distributed over all glued areas. Allow the glue to dry and cure before removing the weights, covering, and tape.

Hems and straight seams in light- to regular-weight fabrics can be glued in the same manner. Press a 1/4-inch seam allowance to the wrong side along the top edge of the hem or one of the adjoining seams. Apply masking tape along the line on the fabric where the hem or two seams will be joined. Apply a light coating of glue on the wrong side of the fabric over the inside and outside of the pressed 1/4-inch seam allowance. Position the hem or seam next to the masking tape. Use either a Clover Needlecraft, Inc. *Finger Presser* or the tip of your finger to secure the bond. Cover the glued areas with either a *Teflon* pressing sheet or cooking parchment paper and place weights along the glued areas. Allow the glue to dry and cure before removing the weights, covering, and tape.

Hems and straight seams in non-raveling fabrics (felt, leather, synthetic suede, etc.) do not require pressing a 1/4-inch seam allowance to the wrong side of the hem or seam. Place masking tape along the line where the hem or two seams will be joined. Apply a 1/4-inch band of glue along the wrong side of the hem or seam. Position the hem or seam next to the masking tape. Use either a Clover Needlecraft Inc. *Finger Presser* or your fingertip to secure the bond.

Brands of permanent fabric glues include:

- **Aleene's** *OK To Wash-It, Platinum Bond Super Fabric Textile Adhesive,* **and** *Flexible Stretchable Fabric Glue*
- **Back Street Inc.** *Border Patrol*
- **Beacon** *Patch Attack*
- **Bond** *Fabric Glue* **and** *Victory 1991*
- **Collins** *Unique Stitch* **and** *Vinyl Repair*
- **Crafter's Pick** *Fabric Glue*
- **Delta** *Stitchless*
- **Dritz** *Liquid Stitch*
- **Eclectic Products** *E-6000*
- **FPC/Surebonder** *Glue It Fabric Adhesive* **and** *Fabric Glue*
- **UHU** *Glu Works Fabric Glue*

Cover the glued areas with either a *Teflon* pressing sheet or cooking parchment paper and place weights along the glued areas. Allow the glue to dry and cure before removing the weights, covering, and tape.

Collins *Unique Stitch* can be used with synthetic fabrics and is excellent for repairing tears and rips in nylon outer wear, including ski wear. Clip loose threads from the edges of the tear. Cut a piece of Sulky Stabilizer (either *Tear-Easy* or *Cut-Away Soft 'n Sheer*) that is 1/2 inch wider and 1/2 inch longer than the tear. Slide the stabilizer into the opening, positioning it so that it is directly behind the tear; pin in place. Apply *Unique Stitch* lightly to each edge of the tear and push the edges together so that the stabilizer is not visible. Brush a light coat of the glue over the junction; allow to dry flat and remove pins. If desired, a fabric appliqué or a small piece of leather can be applied over the

> **Brands of glues suitable for leather and suede include:**
> - Aleene's *Leather and Suede Glue*
> - Bond *Stik*
> - Collins *Unique Stitch*
> - Eclectic Products *E-6000*
> - FPC/Surebonder *Glue It Fabric Adhesive*
>
> **Read and follow the manufacturer's directions for these glues; each differs slightly in the method of application.**

tear with *Unique Stitch*.

In addition to the mentioned fabric glues, other products suitable for stitchless sewing include iron-on fusibles, liquid fusibles, and hot glues described in Chapter 9.

Project

Wedding Purse and Ring Pillow

The beaded lace used for this ring pillow and bride's purse was free! As the wedding dress was altered, the leftover bits and parts and pieces of lace were saved. Fabric glue "stitched" the pieces to a plain satin pillow and purse. Depending upon the amount available, pieces also can be glued to the front of a plain satin guest book and around the base of the accompanying penholder.

> **You Will Need**
> Scrap pieces of lace
> Satin ring pillow
> Satin drawstring purse
> Delta *Stitchless*
> Miscellaneous supplies: pencil, typing or computer paper, small scissors, small brush, straight pins, waxed paper, needle-tip applicator bottle, white twist ties, needle, white thread

1. Sort the pieces of lace according to size and shape. Trace the outline of the pillow on the paper. Trace the outline of the purse on another piece of paper; if covering both sides of the purse, make two tracings (covering both sides of the purse is optional). Set the pillow and purse aside.

2. Arrange the lace pieces on the tracings. Some pieces will overlap; cut away excess so that the lace lies flat on the paper. Clip any loose threads.

3. Beginning with the pieces in the center of the pillow, use the brush to apply a small amount of glue along the back of the pieces. Allow the glue to become slightly tacky, place the pieces on the pillow top, and lightly tap along the glued edge of the piece. Push straight pins through the piece into the pillow to hold the piece in place. Continue adding pieces in this manner until the pillow top is covered with lace; set aside to dry. When dry, remove the pins.

4. Stuff the inside of the purse with wadded pieces of waxed paper. Beginning at the front, glue the lace pieces on the purse in the same manner followed for the pillow. Push straight pins through the pieces into the waxed paper inside the purse to hold them in place until the glue sets. When the front of the purse is covered with lace, set aside to dry. When dry, remove the pins. Turn the purse over and apply lace pieces to the back in the same manner followed for the front. Set aside to dry.

5. When all glue has dried, use the needle-tip applicator bottle to apply very small drops of glue under any lace pieces that are not securely bonded to either the pillow or purse.

6. Fold two (one for a single ring ceremony) white twist ties in half. Open flat and stitch each twist tie over the fold line to either the front or back of the pillow. On the day of the wedding, attach the rings to the pillow with the twist ties. After the ceremony, remove the twist ties by clipping the stitches.

Temporary Stitchless Sewing

Hand basting and/or pinning fabric pieces in place when hand or machine sewing isn't necessary thanks to temporary fabric glue. When dry, Aleene's *No-Sew Fabric Glue*, Crafter's Pick *Basting Glue*, and Sullivan's *Glue Pins* allow for machine stitching through the glue line without gumming up the needle. Hand-stitch adjacent to the glue line. When stitching is completed, launder washable fabric to remove the glue. Each of these products is applied in a slightly different manner; read and follow the manufacturer's directions. **Note:** Crafter's Pick *Basting Glue* is not removed by dry cleaning.

Dritz *Thread Fuse*, a heat-activated thread, is used either for hand or machine basting. When pressed with an iron, the stitching is temporary; laundering removes it from fabrics.

Brands of temporary spray adhesives for fabric are discussed on page 54.

Unlimited Embellishing

Don't limit embellishments to fabric—the variety of glues and adhesives available allow bonding of embellishments to both porous and non-porous surfaces.

Read and follow the manufacturer's directions for the product you have selected, because brands differ in the manner the adhesive is applied. Keep in mind that not every product is suitable for all techniques; some solvent-based products are not recommended for use with acrylic or metal embellishments or for every surface.

Embellishing supplies run the gamut from tiny glass beads the size of a grain of sand to large pieces of tree bark. "Found treasures" (another person's trash) are as popular as purchased supplies.

Glues, adhesives, and dimensional fabric paint bond embellishments to fabric for fast and easy stitchless embellishing. When placing embellishments on fabric that will be either laundered or dry cleaned, select a product that is labeled with laundry and/or dry cleaning instructions. Prepare the fabric as directed for stitchless sewing.

It's difficult to judge correct placement of embellishments when a garment is flat on the work surface. Before applying embellishments to clothing, put the clothing on and place safety pins where you **do not** want embellishments; use an air-erasable marker to mark the locations where you **do** want embellishments.

As directed for fabric glues, use either a shirt board or press a barrier to the back of the fabric before applying paint.

When applying acrylic beads and stones to surfaces that will be laundered and/or dry-cleaned, or to projects that will receive frequent handling, most brands recommend applying a small puddle of glue or paint where the embellishment will be placed; the puddle should be large enough so when the embellishment is pushed into it, the glue or paint oozes up around its base (see below).

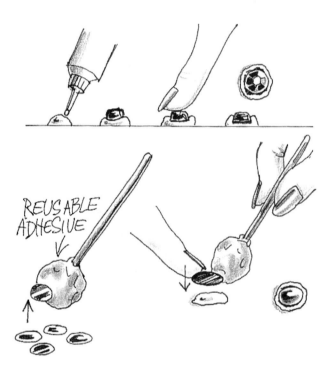

REUSABLE ADHESIVE

A handy picker-upper for positioning embellishments is a small piece of reusable adhesive (Chapter 6) stuck on the end of a manicure orange stick or craft stick. Use either your fingertip or a toothpick to push the embellishment off the adhesive (see above).

Usually a coating of either glue or paint to the back of larger embellishments (buttons, charms, etc.) is enough to secure it to the surface. After the embellishment is positioned, gently push down on it to secure the bond.

There are times when an embellishment is not compatible with the laundering method used for the garment being embellished, for instance an ornate sequin appliqué on a T-shirt. The solution is provided by using a repositionable glue or adhesive. FPC/Surebonder *Moveable Adhesive* is formulated for this technique. Other repositionable glues are described in Chapter 6, and repositionable pressure sensitive adhesive films are described in Chapter 7.

If the backing of the embellishment is fragile or very thin, apply Sulky *Sticky,* a self-adhesive stabilizer, to the back of the embellishment before applying the repositionable product. The stabilizer will prevent the repositionable product from seeping through to the front of the embellishment. After wearing the garment, remove the embellishment as soon as possible; if left in place on the garment, the embellishment may become permanently bonded. Store embellishments flat on the shiny side of freezer paper or a piece of transparency film.

Art Accents *Beedz*, small glass beads without holes, introduced rubber stampers to stitchless beading. It wasn't long before non-stampers realized how quickly and easily small beads could be applied to surfaces other than paper. Magicalfaerieland *Faerie Glass*, tiny glass beads, also are used on all surfaces. Glitter is available in an almost endless array of colors and sizes. Once considered primarily for fabric, all surfaces are now fair game for glitter.

A Helmac *Pick-Up* by Dritz quickly cleans up small beads, glitter, and embossing powder from work surfaces. One roll over the surface and the mess is gone (provided, of course, you didn't spill a full jar). Another handy picker-upper is a piece of removable adhesive. Roll the adhesive into a "snake" and roll it over the work surface.

Brands of dimensional fabric paints include:
- DecoArt
- Delta
- Dr. Ph. Martin
- Jones Tones
- Plaid
- Scribbles
- Tulip

Brands of glues and adhesives suitable for bonding embellishments include:
- Aleene's *Jewel-It* and *Platinum Bond Super Fabric Textile Adhesive*
- Art Accents *Shimmerz*
- The Art Institute *Glittering System Designer "Dries Clear" Adhesive, Designer "Dries White" Adhesive*, and *Fabric "Dried Clear" Adhesive*
- Beacon *Gem Tac*
- Bond *CoolGloo* (cartridge for use in *Cool-Bonder Applicator*), *527 Multi-Purpose Cement*, and *Victory 1991*
- Collins *Vinyl Repair*
- Crafter's Pick *Jewel Glue* and *Ultimate*
- Eclectic *E-6000*
- FPC/Surebonder *Glue It Fabric Adhesive*
- Hot glues (Chapter 9)
- Jones Tones *Plexi 400*
- Liquid repositionable adhesives (Chapter 6)
- Lucky Squirrel *Ultra Thin Bond*
- Pressure sensitive adhesives (Chapter 7)
- USArt Quest *Perfect Paper Adhesive*
- Warm Country *Beads-2-Fuse*
- What's New *Fuse O Bond*
- White and tacky glues (Chapter 2)

Wood

Although most all-purpose white (PVA) glues can be used with wood crafting, glues specifically formulated for wood offer features not found in an all-purpose glue. Wood glues are found in water-based (natural and synthetic-based) and solvent-based products, in addition to pressure sensitive adhesives and hot glues.

The end use of the project, the size of the pieces involved, and the type of product you prefer determine which product is best suited for use. The label of each product will list suitable uses, if the product is solvent-based, and the time required for curing.

A common error is to assume that every wood glue is suitable for objects that remain outdoors. "Water-proof" or "weather-resistant" will be on the label for products that offer those features. "Water-resistant" indicates that the product will withstand exposure to moisture; however, the bond will weaken if submerged in water or exposed to moisture for long periods of time. Products labeled "water-reversible" should not be exposed to extreme moisture.

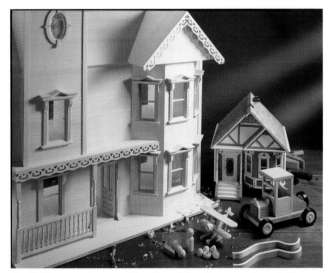

Doll House, designed by Franklin International. It's unlikely anyone would not enjoy being the owner of this house. It certainly isn't a "quickie" project—construction and decoration could take as long as a people-sized home. But when completed, it would be as appreciated and enjoyed as much as the real thing.

Water-based wood glues generally have a longer set and cure time than solvent-based glues. Regardless of the type of glue you select, do not use the item until the glue or adhesive has reached full cure. Low temperatures and/or high humidity will extend the time required for curing.

Wood glues that are clear or white in the container dry almost clear, those that are yellow or beige dry close to that color, and those in wood tones dry to that color.

The surface of the wood should be clean, dry, and free of oil, grease, and dust before applying either glue or an adhesive. In general, wood should be lightly sanded, then wiped clean of dust before beginning. This is particularly important if the wood was previously waxed, sealed, painted, or varnished. Wood that has been oiled should be wiped off with a solvent cleaner and dried before sanding. Avoid green wood; it does not bond well and usually warps.

Clamping or weighting usually is recommended by manufacturers. Apply pressure slowly to ensure correct alignment of the pieces. If using clamps, protect the areas under them with pieces of felt or fabric. *Amazing Wonder Tape* (available from Clotilde) is a handy supply to use when clamps are not suitable. The tape is similar to cling vinyl and leaves no adhesive residue on surfaces.

Use a damp cotton swab to remove any glue or adhesive that oozes from the junctions as pieces are clamped or tied in place. If necessary, use an emery board or fine sand paper to lightly sand away any lingering residue.

When using a contact glue or cement, follow the manufacturer's directions for the product you have selected; the directions vary slightly for each brand. All require that the glue or cement is applied to both surfaces and allowed to dry to a certain state before the surfaces are placed together. Most require that the surfaces are clamped, tied, and/or weighted after being joined together.

Instructions for polyurethane glues often direct you to wipe off the involved surfaces with a dampened sponge or cloth. Don't be surprise if the glue foams as it sets; that's the nature of this type of glue.

Water-based products include:
- **Crafter's Pick Sand-N-Stain**
- **Delta** *Woodwiz*
- **Elmer's** *Carpenter's Wood Glue*
- **FPC/Surebonder** *Professional Wood Glue*
- **Franklin International** *Titebond Liquid Hide Glue*
- **LePages** *Original Glue*
- **Roo Products, Inc.** *RooWood Glue* **and** *RooTac*

In addition to instant glues, the following products described in Chapter 10 require you to follow certain precautions:
- **Aleene's** *Platinum Bond Patio & Garden* **and** *Platinum Bond 7800*
- **Bond** *CoolGloo* **(cartridge for use in** *Cool-Bonder Applicator***)**
- **Eclectic** *E-6000*
- **Elmer's** *Stix-All*
- **FPC/Surebonder** *CG-9000* **(cartridge for use in** *Cool Glue Gun***) and** *9000 Adhesive & Sealant*
- **Franklin International** *Original Wood Glue, Premium - Titebond II, Wood Molding Glue, Polyurethane Glue,* **and** *Dark Wood Glue*
- **Great Planes** *Pro Wood Glue* **(available from Tower Hobbies)**
- **Quick Grab Inc.** *Quick Grab, Quick Grab Silicone* **(clear), and** *Quick Plumbers Silicone* **(white)**
- **UHU** *All Purpose Glue, Contact Cement Stic, Plastic Repair Glue,* **and** *Model & Hobby Glue*

Project

Driftwood Wreath

Designed by Gilbert Davis

The driftwood for this wreath was gathered on the shores of Lake Superior. If you don't have access to a beach, most crafts store have bags of driftwood. Note that this wreath is not intended for outdoor display.

> ### You Will Need
> Circular frame made from paneling scrap or 1/4-inch plywood (lumber yards will cut a plywood frame) in the diameter of your choice
> Driftwood
> Elmer's *Carpenter's Wood Glue*
> Hanger for back of wreath
> Miscellaneous supplies: craft stick, pencil, paper

1. Sort the driftwood pieces according to size and shape. Trace the frame shape on the paper. Arrange the driftwood pieces on the tracing in a pleasing design; several will overlap.
2. Using the craft stick, apply the *Carpenter's Wood Glue* to the back of the driftwood pieces, bond the driftwood to the frame. Allow to dry.
3. Attach a hanger to the back of the frame.

Polymer Clay

There's no question that polymer clay is one of the more difficult surfaces for bonding. Solvent-based adhesives offer one solution when a strong bond is required, for instance pin backs.

One water-based glue that works well for bonding polymer clay is Crafter's Pick *"The Ultimate."* When used with polymer clay, it is used as a contact glue: apply *"The Ultimate"* to both surfaces being joined, allow to dry until almost clear (some streaks of white still will be visible), and tightly press the two surfaces together, holding the surfaces together until the bond is secure. Allow to cure for 24 hours.

When a porous surface (wood, clay flower pots, mat board, etc.) is covered with the clay, the porous surface must be coated with a water-based white glue (Delta *Sobo* is often used) prior to covering it with uncured clay.

The porous surface must be completely dry before being coated with the water-based glue. To ensure that dryness, place the porous item in a warm oven (200 degrees) for 15 minutes. Allow to cool, then coat with the glue. Allow the glue to reach set; it will be almost clear. Apply the clay over the glue. Cure (bake) the clay as directed by the manufacturer.

Of the products described in Chapter 10, instant glues are probably most frequently selected for use with polymer clay. When both surfaces are not smooth and flat, one that is labeled "gap filling" (usually a gel) provides the best results. Instant glue accelerators (use the same brand of accelerator and glue) also eliminate bonding problems when the two surfaces being bonded are not flush.

Products often selected by polymer clay artists include:
- **Bond Victory 1991 (suitable for bonding clay pieces not placed under heavy stress)**
- **Eclectic Products *E-6000***
- **FPC/Surebonder *9000 Adhesive & Sealant***
- **Satellite City *Hot Stuff, Special-T Hot Stuff*, and *Super-T Hot Stuff***
- **SuperHold *"Drip-Proof, Clog-Proof" Super Glue***

The clay must be cured and cool before applying these adhesives.

Two Ways to Attach a Pin Back to Polymer Clay

Adhesive

When bonding pin backs with a liquid adhesive, make an impression of the pin's base in the back of the clay prior to curing. Don't make the impression too deep; the workings of hinge and clasp should not be hindered. After the clay has been cured and is cool, apply the adhesive as directed by the manufacturer (either to both the clay and pin back, or to one surface only) and position it in the impression.

Lucky Squirrel *Ultra Thin Bond*, a heat-activated adhesive film, can be used to apply pin backs to polymer clay. After the clay has been cured and is cool, apply a coat of a polymer clay finish (American Art Clay *Fimo Varnish* or Polyform *Sculpey Glaze*) to the back of the pin. Allow to dry then apply a second coat; allow to dry. Use fine sand paper to lightly sand the area where the pin back will be placed. Dampen a cotton swab slightly with rubbing alcohol and wipe across the sanded area. Allow to dry before applying *Ultra Thin Bond*.

Pressure sensitive adhesive film (Chapter 7) with a heavy tack can be used to bond embellishments made from polymer clay to surfaces that are not frequently handled (collages, picture frames, holiday decorations, etc.). Follow the method described above for *Ultra Thin Bond*.

Liquid Sculpey

Although not an adhesive, Polyform *Liquid Sculpey* often is used for bonding pieces of polymer clay together and for applying pin backs. A thin coat of *Liquid Sculpey* is brushed to one side of the pieces of a clay design that will be joined together (i.e. the arms and legs of a figure). The pieces are joined together and allowed to sit for up to six hours. Before curing, re-check the alignment of the pieces. Cure at the temperature and time as directed on the clay packaging.

To secure a pin back to clay, make an impression in the back of the clay with the pin back. Pick up the pin back and brush a thin coat of *Liquid Sculpey* into the impression. Replace the pin into the impression. Cut a small piece of clay to cover the exposed base of the pin back. The piece of clay should extend slightly beyond each of the long edges of the pin back, but it should not be too thick or wide to interfere with the hinge or clasp of the pin back.

Pick up the small piece of clay and brush a thin coat of *Liquid Sculpey* over the back of it and place the coated side over the pin back. Gently smooth the edges of the piece to the back of the clay. Allow to sit for six hours. Before curing the clay, lightly smooth the clay covering the pin back to secure the bond. Cure at the temperature and time as directed on the clay packaging.

If the stress placed on a junction of pieces will not be great, or if the finished piece will not be handled frequently, polymer clay pieces can be bonded together without an adhesive. Join the two pieces together and allow to sit for 24 hours. Check the alignment of the pieces prior to curing at the temperature and time recommended by the clay manufacturer.

Project

Glorious Candlestick

Designed by Barbara A. McGuire, Creative Claystamps

A plain wooden candlestick quickly becomes glorious with the addition of polymer clay and metallic leaf… somewhat like the ugly duckling turning into a beautiful swan.

You Will Need

Wooden candlestick (unfinished)
1/2 block *Fimo* soft: Black #9*
One sheet *Magic Leaf*: Sea Blue*
One sheet *Magic Leaf*: Gold*
*Magic Leaf Adhesive**
Crafter's Pick *"The Ultimate"*
Design Innovations Chinese Writing
    Stamp ©Creative Claystamps
    (designed by Nan Roche)
Card stock for working and baking
    surface
Acrylic brayer or rolling pin*
Oven
600 Grit wet sandpaper or manicure
    sanding block
*Fimo Varnish**
*Magic Leaf Varnish**
Miscellaneous supplies: Sharp blade,
    application brush, scissors, small
    brushes, small cloth
Optional: pasta machine

*Available from Accent Import-Export, Inc.

1. Brush *"The Ultimate"* over the areas of the candlestick to which polymer clay will be applied. Allow to dry.
2. Condition the clay by kneading it in your hands until soft and pliable. If using a pasta machine, run thinly sliced slabs through the machine starting at setting #1 and decreasing to setting #5; fold and repeat seven passes through the machine.
3. Make a flat sheet of clay that is approximately 1/8-inch thick and slightly larger than the size needed to cover the candle stick. Use the brayer to flatten the sheet so that it is even, or stack two sheets that were run through the pasta machine at #1 setting. Place the clay on the card stock.
4. Cut a portion of the Sea Blue metal leaf and place it directly on the clay. Using your fingers, smooth and secure the leaf to the clay (glue will not be needed).
5. Press the "mold" side (not the rubber side) of the stamp into the clay strip; push with enough force to impress the design in the clay. The leaf will prevent the stamp from sticking to the clay.

6. Wrap the embossed clay around the candlestick over the areas where the glue was applied. Trim away excess clay from areas not to be decorated.
7. Bake the clay according to the manufacturer's directions. *Fimo* cures at an oven temperature of 265 degrees F; baking should be complete in 20 minutes. Remove from the oven and allow to cool.
8. Gently sand the leaf off the raised portion of the design. Wipe off the clay with a damp cloth; allow to dry. Varnish the clay portion of the candlestick.
9. Referring to the photo, brush *Magic Leaf Adhesive* over the areas to be covered with gold leaf. Allow to dry to a tacky state. Apply the leaf to the adhesive. It may be necessary to use a small brush to apply the leaf around the curved edges of the candlestick.
10. Brush *Magic Leaf Varnish* over all leafed areas.

Glass

The project's end use is the deciding factor when selecting an adhesive for glass. Decorative objects that will receive limited handling do not require an adhesive that forms a strong bond, while objects intended for heavy use (i.e. paper weights, jewelry, etc.) require an adhesive that will withstand frequent handling. Read the label of the product you have selected to ensure it is suitable for the project you are doing.

Some products can be used for bonding porous surfaces to glass. To ensure good bonding, wipe off glass with either the supply recommended by the glue or adhesive manufacturer or rubbing alcohol. Allow the glass to dry before applying glue or adhesive.

Products formulated for bonding paper and fabric to glass include:
- Aabbitt Adhesives, Inc. *Super 88*
- Aleene's *Instant Decoupage* and *Reverse Collage* glue
- Art Accents *Shimmerz*
- Back Street, Inc. *Anita's Decoupage Glue*
- Beacon *Gem Tac* and *Liquid Laminate*
- Crafter's Pick *"The Ultimate"*
- Plaid *Mod Podge* and Royal Coat *Decoupage Finish* (also a glue)

These products also provide a protective finish that can be wiped off with a damp cloth, but should not be immersed in water. (See Chapter 3 for additional decoupage techniques.)

ColArt Americas, Inc. *Tile and Glass Colors*, a decorative glass paint, is suitable for bonding glass pieces and beads to other glass surfaces. To ensure a strong bond, bake the finished piece as directed on the label. ColArt Americas, Inc. *Tile and Glass Colors Simulated Lead Adhesive* also bonds glass to glass. Available in silver and gold, the adhesive is packaged in an applicator tube.

Silicone-based adhesives and silicone sealants are waterproof and weather-resistant, making them an excellent choice for just about any project that will be left out of doors. Although there are few surfaces that cannot be bonded with silicone, neither the adhesives nor sealants can be painted or varnished. Read and follow all manufacturer's directions; cure time may exceed 24 hours.

In addition to those previously mentioned, other products suitable for bonding glass include:
- Aleene's *Platinum Bond 7800*
- Bond *527* and *Victory 1991*
- FPC/Surebonder *9000 Adhesive & Sealant*
- Germanow & Simon *G-S Cement*
- National Art Glass *All Hold* and *Glass Hold*
- Plaid *Make It Mosaics Adhesive*
- UHU *Plastic Repair Glue* and *Model & Hobby Glue*

Project

Decoupage Plate

Designed by Stacy Nelson, Bellarosa Paper Arts

This beautiful plate would be a stunning addition to any room. It's hard to believe it's such an easy project.

You Will Need
Clear glass plate, 8-inch diameter
Plaid *Mod Podge*
Gold leaf sheets
Leaf adhesive size
Bellarosa Paper Arts *Decoupage/Collage Papers, Victorian Paper Ephemera*
Tissue paper: Gold
Flat brush for *Mod Podge*
Small, soft brush for applying leaf adhesive size
Soft brush for leaf sheets
Small scissors with sharp points
Miscellaneous supplies: paper, pencil, rubbing alcohol, small cloth

1. Trace the plate on the paper. Remove the plate and set side. Select the images that will be used for the plate, having one as a focal point. Cut out all of the images. To avoid having white areas around the cut edges, tilt your cutting hand so the palm is slightly up when cutting. When cutting, rotate the image, rather than the scissors.
2. Arrange the images, face up, on the plate tracing. Leave open areas from the inner rim of the plate to the center for the gold leaf.

3. Wipe off the back of the plate with rubbing alcohol; allow to dry. Apply *Mod Podge* to the front of the main image. Position the image on the back of the plate; gently press in place with your fingertips. Apply *Mod Podge* to the front of the images surrounding the base of the focal image and position on the place. Gently press in place with your fingertips. Turn the plate over, right side up; all pieces should be smooth and flat. Turn the plate over so that the back is up.

4. Add the images around the inner rim of the plate in the same manner followed in Step 3. It is not necessary that the images overlap one another; however, all should be facing the same direction. Leaving the plate back up, allow the glue to dry.

5. Apply leaf adhesive size to the back of the plate to the open areas in the center of the plate. Allow to dry to a tacky state. Lay a sheet of leaf over the adhesive; using the soft brush (it will be dry), gently tap the leaf to the adhesive. Repeat until all adhesive is covered with leaf.

When the adhesive size is covered, gently brush away excess leaf with the soft brush.

6. Apply the images selected for the area between the inner and outer rim of the plate. Place these images closely together to avoid open areas. All images should be smooth and flat on the plate. Allow to dry.

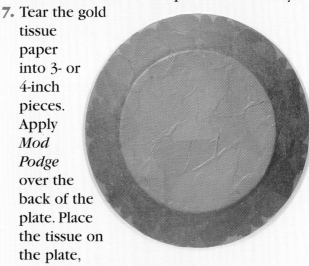

7. Tear the gold tissue paper into 3- or 4-inch pieces. Apply *Mod Podge* over the back of the plate. Place the tissue on the plate, overlapping the pieces. When the back is entirely covered with the tissue, brush a thin coat of *Mod Podge* over it. Allow to dry. Trim away excess tissue from the outer rim of the plate.

Floral Glues

When a container is being used for a floral arrangement, it's usually easier if a base of plastic foam is secured in the container prior to creating the arrangement. Apply glue (test if using a solvent-based product) to the bottom of the foam, then position it in the container. Allow the glue to dry so that the base is stable and secure before beginning.

Skeleton leaves and dried flowers frequently are used to embellish paper projects. To ensure that the color of a skeleton leaf will not bleed to the background paper, or that the glue will not seep through the front of the leaf, apply glue very lightly only along the vein lines and the leaves' outer edges. When using dried flowers, place a drop of glue on the back of the flowers at the widest part. Do not burnish leaves or flowers in place; use your fingertip to gently tap them to the background.

> **In addition to Delta *Floral Glue*, other products suitable for bonding dried and silk flowers include:**
> - **Acrylic-based adhesives (Chapter 5)**
> - **Aleene's *Foamtastic***
> - **Bond *CoolGloo* (cartridge used in *Cool-Bonder Applicator*)**
> - **Crafter's Pick *"The Ultimate"***
> - **Floral hot glues (Chapter 9)**
> - **FPC *Surebonder CG-9000* (cartridge used in *Cool Glue Gun*)**
> - **Tacky glues (Chapter 3)**

Pastes (Chapter 2) and water-based glues, including those that are acrylic-based, can be used to bond leaves and dried flowers to paper; thin bodied solvent-based adhesives and cements are suitable, provided paper is listed as a recommended surface on the label.

STYROFOAM

Acrylic mediums bond *STYROFOAM* pieces and also can be used for surface application; thick-bodied acrylic mediums quickly cover and disguise the uneven surface of the foam. When used as a surface application, the mediums can be colored prior to use, or painted with an acrylic paint when dry. Acrylic mediums and coloring supplies for the mediums are discussed in Chapter 5.

Many solvent-based adhesives and cements melt plastic foams, as do some high-temperature hot glues. If using one of these products, test before beginning.

> **Some products are formulated for STYROFOAM, including:**
> - **Aleene's *Foamtastic***
> - **Beacon *Hold The Foam***
> - **Bond *Foam Glue* (cartridge for use in *CoolBonder Applicator*)**
> - **Tacky glues (Chapter 2) set faster and are less messy than thinner viscosity water-based glues**
> - **Water-based glues, acrylic-based adhesives, and low-temperature hot glues (Chapter 9) also are suitable**

Craft Foam

Here's another difficult surface (it's a close second to polymer clay). Although not often thought of as a craft foam, Sulky of America *Puffy Foam* is available in colors in both 2mm and 3mm thicknesses and is suitable for all craft foam techniques.

> **In addition to Beacon Craft Foam Glue, which is formulated for use with craft foam, other suitable products include double-sided pressure sensitive products, including:**
> - **Aleene's *Photo Memory Glue***
> - **High-tack double-sided adhesives (Chapter 7)**
> - **Repositionable glues**

Apply Aleene's *Photo Memory Glue* to the foam with the brush top included with the bottle. Allow the glue to become slightly tacky before joining the pieces together. It may be necessary to either clamp (paper clips and long bobby pins work for small pieces) or place small weights on the pieces until the glue has dried.

For a repositionable (temporary) hold, use one of the repositionable liquid glues described in Chapter 6. Dimensional stickers are quickly made when a repositionable glue is placed on the back of shapes you purchase pre-cut or make by either cutting or punching. Zig *Textile Markers* (heat setting will not be necessary) can be used for coloring shapes and designs.

Repositionable glues and pressure sensitive adhesive film or tape can be used for applying either craft foil or metal leaf to the surface of craft foam. The glue can be applied either in a light covering coat or heavily, then textured by patting with the side of a brush or craft stick.

Allow the glue to dry to a tacky state before applying either the foil or leaf. If the glue was textured, brush powdered mica pigments over the applied foil or leaf to highlight the texture. Application of an acrylic varnish to the foil or leaf is recommended.

One advantage offered by craft foam is the ease in which it is cut. Scissors, including those with a decorative edge, rotary cutters, and paper cutters quickly cut the foam in desired shapes and designs. The problems encountered when cutting an intricate shape in mat board and foam core for the window of a shaker card are eliminated with craft foam. See pages 66 and 67 for additional uses of craft foam.

Project

Shake, Shake, Shake It!

Craft foam is the secret to this shaker card. It would be very difficult to cut a piece of foam core to duplicate the outer edges of a two-section plastic ornament in this Christmas tree shape.

You Will Need

One section of a plastic ornament

One piece of light-colored 3 mm craft foam that is at least 2 inches longer and wider than the ornament

One piece of mat board that is at least 2 inches longer and wider than the ornament

Three sheets of decorative paper (purchased or self-made): two must be at least 1/2 inch wider and longer than the craft foam; one must be at least 1/2 inch wider and longer than the ornament

Three sheets of double-sided adhesive film in the same sizes as the decorative paper

1/4-inch wide double-sided adhesive tape with liner

Piece of trim cord long enough to encircle the ornament

Shakers (plastic spangles were used in the example)

Repositionable glue in applicator bottle

Stamp pad: black

Miscellaneous supplies: scissors, craft knife or rotary cutter, mat and ruler, pencil, small ruler, burnishing tool

Step 10 is optional; small piece of white craft foam, Clearsnap, Inc. *Crafter's Ink*, Zig *Textile Markers*, Rollagraph Never Enough ©Clearsnap, Inc. and Brushed Star ©Stampendous

1. Place one section of the ornament on the work surface with the back up. Pat the stamp pad on the edges of the ornament. Place the ornament, inked edges down, in the center of the craft foam. When the ornament is lifted from the craft foam, there should be a clear imprint of the edges of the ornament on the craft foam. Cut along the lines of the imprint to create an opening in the foam that is the same shape and size of the ornament section. Set the ornament aside.

2. Using either a craft knife or rotary cutter, cut the craft foam so that it is approximately 1 inch wider on each side and 1-1/2 inches longer at each end than the opening. Cut the mat board and two pieces of double-stick adhesive film to the same size as the craft foam. Set the mat board aside.

3. Place one piece of adhesive film on the work surface, release paper side up. Place the craft foam on the adhesive film. Using the pencil, trace the opening on the release paper. Pick up the craft foam. Trace a line 1/2 inch toward the center of the first tracing (this tracing will be the same shape as the opening, but smaller). Cut along the second traced line.

4. Remove the release paper from the adhesive film. Position the cut piece of adhesive film over the front of the craft foam. Secure the edges of the film over the inside edges of the opening with your fingertip. It may be necessary to make small slashes along the edges of the film if the opening is curved. Leaving the liner in place, burnish the film in place on the foam.

5. Cut two pieces of decorative paper that are 1/2 inch wider and 1/2 inch longer than the mat board. Set aside. Place strips of the 1/4-inch tape along all outer edges of the back (the side without the adhesive film) of the craft foam; leave the liner in place. Place 1/4-inch tape along all edges of one side of the mat board; place adhesive film on the other side of the mat board. This side will be the back of the mat board.

6. Remove the liner from the adhesive film on the mat board. Position one piece of the decorative paper on the adhesive film. Bring the edges up over the front of the board and crease the excess paper along the edges of the craft foam. Remove the liner from the tape on the front of the board. Secure the edges of the decorative paper to the tape.

7. Place the craft foam on the front of the mat board. Trace the opening of the craft foam onto the front of the mat board. Place a piece of adhesive film over the traced area. Cover with a piece of decorative paper. This paper will be visible through the front of the ornament.

8. Remove the liner from the adhesive film covering the front of the craft foam. Cover the film with the second piece of decorative paper. Cut out the opening, leaving a 1/4-inch allowance to wrap to the back of the opening. Turn the craft foam over. Place 1/4-inch tape around the edges of the opening. Remove the liner and secure the paper to the tape. Place 1/4-inch adhesive tape along the four outer edges of the craft foam. Place the craft foam on the front of the mat board. Burnish to secure the craft foam to the mat board.

9. Place the selected "shakers" in the opening of the craft foam. Position the ornament in the opening. Apply repositionable glue along the edges of the ornament. Immediately place the trim cord around the base of the ornament. Press firmly to secure the trim to the ornament.

10. (Optional) In the example, adhesive film was applied to the back of a piece of white craft foam. A *Rollagraph* design was printed on the front of the craft foam with Clearsnap, Inc. *Crafter's Ink.* The ink was heat set with a heat gun held 6 inches from the foam. The print was colored with *Textile Markers.* The print was cut apart, the liner was removed from the adhesive film, and the pieces were placed below the tree. The star was made in the same manner.

Leave the release paper in place until after designs and/or shapes have been cut or punched out when either a permanent or repositionable pressure sensitive adhesive film has been applied to the back of the foam, or when using Darice *Sticky-Back Foamies*; the foam must be cut or punched before applying *Sticky Dots Adhesives Sheets* or *Tape* to the back of the pieces. Techniques using craft foam in this way are included in Chapter 7.

Sulky *Sticky,* a self-adhesive stabilizer, provides the solution when you want to decorate the surface of craft foam. The stabilizer provides a surface that is easily decorated with acrylic paints, in addition to water-based coloring supplies (dye re-inkers, markers, etc.). Decorate the stabilizer either before it is placed on the foam or after. Burnish the stabilizer to ensure the bond.

Another option is to apply a high-tack pressure sensitive adhesive film to the back of paper, either one you decorate or purchase decorated. The paper can then be placed on the foam. Burnish the paper to secure the bond.

Metal, Including Wire

The end use of the project and the surfaces involved determine the adhesive used. Jewelry composed of non-porous items (i.e. metal and glass beads) requires a product that forms a very strong bond. Decorative pieces composed of porous and non-porous items (i.e. wood and metal) can be used with a product that forms a medium to light bond.

Metal and wire should be clean, dry, and free of oil and grease. Wipe off surfaces either with the product recommended by the adhesive manufacturer, rubbing alcohol, or vinegar diluted with an equal amount of water. Allow to dry before applying the adhesive.

In general, water-based adhesives do not bond metal to metal. Those that do will include metal and/or wire in the list of recommended surfaces included on the label. Crafter's Pick *"The Ultimate"* can be used for projects that do not require a strong bond. Some acrylic mediums and acrylic-based adhesives also can be used for light bonding; many are suitable only if one surface is porous. Some glues and adhesives require that the metal is sealed with a metal

primer prior to application. Information concerning these requirements will be included on the label of the adhesive product.

Most solvent-based adhesives and cements are suitable for use with metal and wire; read the label to ensure the product you have selected lists metal and wire as a recommended surfaces.

Of the solvent-based products described in Chapter 10, epoxy forms the strongest bond, followed by instant glues. Several products form a medium bond. Germanow-Simon Corp. *G-S Cement* is packaged in a tube having a precision applicator tip, allowing for the exact placement of small drops of glue.

Regardless of which solvent-based product you select, apply only the needed amount; excessive amounts often reduce the bonding ability provided by these products. Read and carefully follow all manufacturer's directions and warnings.

Paper

Paper categories range from the thinnest tissue to mat board. Most are very porous and are easily bonded without problem. It's important to keep in mind that not all papers are colorfast. When a liquid glue is applied to paper that is not colorfast, the color bleeds from the paper into the glue. The glue becomes colored, making it very visible through transparent and translucent papers.

Wipe a damp cotton swab over the front of the paper; if the swab picks up color, the paper is not colorfast. A fixative applied to the front of the paper will prevent bleeding, but a fixative is not needed when a pressure sensitive adhesive is used.

Most metallic papers have a paper backing. For those that don't, repositionable glues used with craft foil and metal leaf, pressure sensitive adhesive films and tapes, jewel glues, and glues recommended for non-porous surfaces can be used to bond these papers to surfaces.

Doll house makers have long known the value of a wallpaper sample book. But the secret is out, and it seems everyone is finding ways to put the papers in the books to good use. They're excellent background papers for paper art; another popular use is self-made envelopes. One adhesive that works especially well is UHU *WallPaper Glue*. Suitable for all types of wallpaper, the glue forms a strong bond that is water-resistant.

Then there's vellum! The problem is not finding a glue or adhesive that bonds vellum, the problem is finding one that does not show through the translucent paper. The variations found in different brands of vellum also complicate the issue—what works well with one brand may not provide the same results with another. When working with vellum or any translucent paper, always test.

One solution is to place a pressure sensitive adhesive film over the entire back of the paper. An acid-free PSA is a lighter-weight adhesive and offers the best results; however, this doesn't provide the solution for projects having the vellum secured only along the top edge.

Therm O Web *Keep-A-Memory Acid Free Mounting Adhesive Tape* (1/4-inch wide) and Scotch *Photo & Document Mounting Tape* (1/2-inch wide) are rarely visible through most brands of vellum. In some cases, results are better if the tape is placed on the background and the vellum is then applied to the tape. Cover the vellum with a scrap piece of vellum and burnish to secure the bond.

In addition to the mentioned tapes, Tombow *Photo Glue Stick*, Judi-Kins *Diamond Glaze*, Plaid *Royal Coat Dimensional Magic*, and USArt Quest *Perfect Paper Adhesive* are not visible through most brands of vellum. Apply only the amount needed for a secure bond; burnish as directed above.

Another solution is to apply a narrow band of an adhesive that does show through to the top edge of the vellum. After positioning the vellum on the adhesive, apply another band of adhesive to the front of the vellum, and cover with an embellishment (i.e. lace, ribbon, small beads, glitter, embossing powder, etc.). The disadvantage of this method is that the added embellishment can over-power a design on the vellum.

Clear and colored photo corners often are used to attach vellum to a background; the size selected is determined by the size of the vellum. Stickers offer another option.

It's not uncommon that a card is designed for display upon receipt. Mat board is used as the background surface; a stick-on easel (Art Accents, Plaid, etc.), included in the envelope, allows the recipient to easily display the card. To bond vellum to a card of this type, cut a piece that is as wide as the mat board, and twice as long. Apply an acid-free pressure sensitive adhesive film to the back of the mat board. Remove the release paper and position the vellum on the film. Bring the vellum up over the front of the card. Place a scrap piece of vellum over the vellum on the top edge of the mat board; burnish to score the vellum so that it folds over the top edge of the mat board.

Paper Cutting Tips:
- Cutting paper doesn't damage or dull scissors or rotary blades, unless the paper is recycled and contains metal.
- Rotary cutters, paper cutters, paper trimmers, craft knives, and the *Olo Rolling Scissors* from Olfa provide the best results for long, straight cuts in paper. Either a rotary ruler or a ruler with a metal edge is necessary when cutting with rotary cutters, craft knives and the *Olo Rolling Scissors*.
- When cutting out shapes and designs, especially those that are curved, use a small sewing scissors with sharp points. Cut away excess before cutting close to the edges of a shape or design. Keep the scissors steady and pointed directly in front of you; rotate the shape, not the scissors, as you cut.
- June Tailor *Quilting Templates* are available in a wide range of shapes and sizes and are excellent for tracing on all surfaces. Fiskars *Circle* and *Oval Cutters*, the *Circle Cutter* from Clotilde, and *Coluzzle* from Provo quickly and accurately cut shapes and/or designs in paper.

The most difficult application is one in which the vellum completely covers either both sides of the outside or the inside of a folded card. The glue or pressure sensitive adhesive tape applied along the folded edge should not be visible, but must still provide adequate bonding so the vellum does not become disengaged from the card.

Brands of glues or pressure sensitive adhesive tape that work well for this technique include:
- Judi-Kins *Diamond Glaze*
- Plaid *Royal Coat Dimensional Magic*
- Sailor *Rolling Ball Glue Pen*
- Scotch *Double-Stick Adhesive Pen*
- Therm O Web *Keep-A-Memory Acid-Free Mounting Adhesive Tape*
- Tombow *Photo Glue Stick*
- UHU *Photo Glue Stick*

For either outside or inside vellum placement on a card, cut a piece of vellum and a piece of card stock to the same size. Score and fold the card stock along the scored line do not burnish the fold line. Place the vellum on the card stock, all edges of the two papers being even. Lightly crease the fold line in the vellum.

For outside placement: Remove the vellum from the card stock. If using a glue stick, leave the card stock folded. Twist up the glue so that it is just barely over the top of the tube; lightly run the folded edge of the card stock across the top of the glue. If using either a liquid glue or pressure sensitive tape, open the vellum flat, with the inside of the fold up. Apply a liquid glue in a thin bead along the fold of the vellum; position tape so that it is centered in the fold.

Position the interior of the vellum fold along the exterior of the card stock fold. Place the card on a flat surface; cover the fold on the vellum with a piece of scrap vellum and burnish to secure the bond. Remove the scrap vellum. If

Handmade Books, designed by Sue Gidduck. Book making is rapidly becoming one of the more popular paper art activities. Sue has contributed greatly to this growth. Her innovative use of supplies and materials, in addition to her beautiful designs, are an inspiration to all. Brown kraft paper was bonded to mat board with Beacon Fabric Tac for the covers of these books. Color was added by either brushing or sponging Plaid Glaze Vernis over the kraft paper. The pages are hand made paper. Japanese stab stitching formed the binding; fibers are from Sue's company, Sueperstuff. More of Sue's designs can be seen at her website (www.sueperstuff.com).

a glue stick or liquid glue was used, allow to dry (approximately 30 minutes).

For inside placement: Remove the vellum from the card stock. If using a glue stick, leave the vellum folded and apply to the folded edge as directed for card stock. If using either a liquid glue or pressure sensitive tape, open the card stock flat. Apply the glue or tape to the interior fold in the same manner as directed for outside placement.

Position the exterior of the vellum fold along the interior of the card stock fold. Run the edge of a charge card down the fold in the vellum to secure it to the card stock. Place the folded card on a flat surface and burnish the folded edge; allow to dry as directed for outside placement.

Jim Stephan *Note Pad Cement* applied along the edge of a stack of cut papers quickly creates small note pads. Decorated or plain, the pads are great little gifts that are sure to delight and impress the recipient. Instructions for making pads are included on the label.

Miscellaneous Surfaces
Plaster

In addition to Plaid *Faster Plaster Glue*, which is formulated for plaster, tacky glues, acrylic-based adhesives, and thicker acrylic mediums can be used for bonding plaster to plaster and plaster to porous and other semi-porous surfaces. When bonding plaster to non-porous surfaces, select an adhesive suitable for the non-porous surface. Test before using a solvent-based adhesive; some may affect the plaster.

Paper Clays

When dry, the surface of clays of this type are porous; adhesives suitable for porous surfaces can be used to bond these clays to other porous surfaces. When bonding to semi-porous and non-porous surfaces, select an adhesive suitable for the surface the clay is being bonded to. In almost every case, a silicone adhesive can be used. Test solvent-based adhesives before use; some may affect the clay.

Mounting Rubber and Polymer Stamps

As noted in earlier chapters, several supplies are suitable for mounting dies to a block, either permanently or temporarily. For those who prefer a cushion under the die, Jim Stephan offers *Double Sticky Cushion*. Each side of the cushion has a very high-tack adhesive when a permanent mount is desired. If a cushion is not desired, any of the double-stick, high-tack adhesive films mentioned in Chapter 7 can be used on the back of a die to permanently mount it on a block. Before applying either *Double Sticky Cushion* or an adhesive film, wipe off the back of the die and the block (wood or acrylic) with a half and half solution of vinegar and water. Allow to dry.

Temporary mounting of stamps is becoming more and more popular. As a stamp collection grows (and it does), storage of mounted stamps becomes a problem. Unmounted dies are easily stored in folders, CD cases, and envelopes. Wood and acrylic blocks are used for temporary mounting. Wipe off the back of the die and the block (wood or acrylic) with a half and half solution of vinegar and water. Allow to dry. Liquid repositionable glues (Chapter 6) and low-tack and repositionable adhesive films and tapes (Chapter 7) can be used for temporarily mounting.

A piece of Grafix *Prepared Frisket Film* placed on the block prior to temporary mounting (wood blocks must be sealed and smooth) eliminates cleaning adhesive residue from the block. As the *Film* becomes sticky or gooey, simply replace it with a clean piece. The *Film* also prevents stains on wood blocks when permanent inks are used. Additional uses for this product are described in Chapter 7.

Resources

With few exceptions, products mentioned in the book are available in one or more of the following catalogs.

ArtLex
(www.artlex.com)
Comprehensive visual arts dictionary

Clotilde
1-800-772-2891 (US)
573-754-7979 (outside US)
On-line ordering (www.clotilde.com/store)
Paper catalog. Comprehensive sewing supplies, extensive crafts supplies; informative catalog

Creative Express
1-800-563-8679
On-line ordering (www.creativexpress.com)
Paper catalog. Comprehensive arts and crafts supplies

Daniel Smith Fine Artist's Materials
1-800-426-6740 (US and Canada)
On-line ordering
(http://www.danielsmith.com/intro.html)
Paper catalog. Comprehensive art and crafts supplies; informative catalog and site

Dharma Trading Company
1-800-542-6227 (US and Canada)
415-456-7657 (elsewhere)
On-line ordering (www.dharmatrading.com)
Paper catalog. Comprehensive textile art supplies, fabric and clothing; informative catalog and site

Dick Blick Art Materials
1-800-447-8192 (US)
309-343-6181 (Intl)
On-line ordering (www.dickblick.com/home-page/a/)
Paper catalog. Comprehensive art and crafts supplies

Fascinating Folds
1-800-968-2418
On-line ordering (www.fascinating-folds.com)
Paper catalog. Comprehensive paper arts supplies, glues and adhesives; informative site

Mirkwood Designs
On-line
(www.mirkwooddesigns.com/index.htm)
Large assortment of copyright free ready-to-print templates for cards, envelopes, and boxes; informative site

NASCO
1-800-558-9595 (US and Canada)
920-563-2446 (elsewhere; ask for Export Department)
On-line ordering
(http://www.nascofa.com/prod/Home)
Paper catalog. Comprehensive art and crafts supplies

PB Plastics
1-800-323-4307
On-line ordering
http://www.pbplastics.com/Default.htm
Xyron machines, supplies and accessories

Sax Arts & Crafts
1-800-558-6696
On-line ordering
(http://web.junebox.com/sax/)
Paper catalog. Comprehensive art and crafts supplies

Tower Hobbies
1-800-673-4989 (US)
217-398-3636 (elsewhere)
On-line ordering (www.towerhobbies.com)
(Type: glue, adhesive, trim tape, or heat gun in Search Bar)
Paper catalog. Mention department WWW when ordering catalog, comprehensive model building supplies, extensive cements and instant glues, trim tapes and heat guns

Twinrocker Paper Making Supplies
1-800-757-8946
On-line ordering (www.twinrocker.com)
Paper catalog. Comprehensive paper making supplies and tools, extensive paper arts supplies and tools

University Products, Inc.
1-800-628-1912
On-line ordering (http://archivalsuppliers.com/)
Paper catalog. Comprehensive archival supplies, pastes, glues, adhesives; informative catalog and site

Wackey Wagon's Ladybug
816-580-3434
On-line ordering
(http://www.wackywagon.com)
Extensive arts and crafts supplies, many hard to find items; informative site

Inspirations

The following books provide food for thought, in addition to excellent ideas and techniques. Enjoy!

Bosler, Barb. *Glass Etching Techniques*. B&B Products, Inc. 1995.

Drexler, Joyce. *Sulky Secrets to Successful Stabilizing*. Harbor Heights, FL: Sulky of America. 1998.
——— *Sulky Secrets to Successful Quilting*. Sulky of America. 2000.

Hart, Cynthia. *Scrapbook Workshop*. New York: Workman Publishing. 1998.

La Plantz, Shereen. *Cover To Cover*. Ashville, NC: Lark Books. 1995.

McGuire, Barbara A. *Foundations in Polymer Clay Design*. Iola, WI: Krause Publications. 1999.

Mulari, Mary. *Appliques With Style*. Iola, WI: Krause Publications. 1998.

——— *Denim & Chambray With Style*. Iola, WI: Krause Publications. 1999.

Pickering Rothamel, Sue. *The Art Of Paper Collage*. Sterling Publications Co., Inc. 2000.

Shepard, Lisa. *African Accents: Fabric and Crafts to Decorate Your Home*. Iola, WI: Krause Publications. 1999.

Walter, Cindy. *More Snippet Sensations*. Iola, WI: Krause Publications. 2000.

Ward, Nancy. *Stamping Made Easy*. Iola, WI: Krause Publications. 1994.

Weinberg, Suze. *The Art of Rubber Stamping*. New York: Sterling Publications Co., Inc. 2000.

Young, Tammy. *The Crafter's Guide to Glues*. Iola, WI: Krause Publications, 1995.

Contributing Designers

The following designers and companies generously granted permission for the display of their works in the book. Refer to the page numbers to view their contributions.

Adhesives Technologies:
Floral mirror, page 92

American Traditional Stencils:
Green Patina Maple Leaf Box, page 33

Barb Bosler, B & B Etching Products, Inc:
Decorated Gift Box, page 114

Gilbert Davis:
Driftwood Wreath, page 125

Franklin International:
Doll House, page 123

Chris Hansen:
Stellar Mask, page 25

Sue Giduck, Sueperstuff:
Handmade Books, page 137
Collage Card, page 20

Susan Gillen
photo: Money Makes The World Go Round,
page 112

Jones Tones, Inc.:
Foiled Flower Pot, page 44

Barbara A. McGuire:
Glorious Candle Stick, page 128

Jill Meyer:
Paper Sculpture, page 32

Mary Mulari, Mary's Productions:
Quickie Banners, page 104

Stacy Nelson:
Decoupage Plate, page 130

Pioneer Photo Albums:
Wedding Album page, page 83

Susan Pickering Rothamel:
And, it was written, page 43

Colleen Rundgun for American Traditional
Stencils:
"Home Tweet Home" Album Page, page 88

Donna Thomason:
Computer Pals, page 94

Victoria Waller:
Pin Beaded Cushion, page 111

Index